A GREATER LIFE AWAITS

Helpful insights for finding and living your bliss

DAKOTA WINDANCER

ISBN 978-1-64349-820-1 (paperback)
ISBN 978-1-64349-821-8 (digital)

Christian Faith Publishing, Inc.
832 Park Avenue
Meadville, PA 16335
www.christianfaithpublishing.com

Printed in the United States of America

To El Shaddai, whose breath is my blessing, and
who I often find in the last place I look…

For Grandmother, who taught me how to read . . .

For Dr. Robert Moore, who taught
me what books to read that gave deep
understanding of my soul's language . . .

For Sparrow, who mentored my metanoia
while in the wasteland of soul . . .

**"If we are wise, we mentor where we are needed,
and allow for mentoring when its needed."**

—Dakota Michael Windancer

Acknowledgments

As it takes a village to raise a child, it also takes comparable networking for bringing a book to its fruition. Therefore, I wish to thank and acknowledge the following institutions and individuals for their inspiration, wisdom, and help in this offering:

My deep gratitude to **The Mankind Project** whose worldwide organization helped me to develop my life's mission. **Shadow Work Inc.** for their facilitation of my own *shadow's* work and teachings.

My deep appreciation to Victoria Dilling for your amazing artwork that is the front and back cover, the beginning and ending of my story.

I cannot emphasize enough the value of my friend and mentor "Conchalele Bob," whose guidance gave form to my internal "juice" and would never have made the page without his help.

Thank you to my good friends Jesse and Mark for their photographic contributions.

I wish to thank Gary also for his gentle encouragement and advice.

My thanks to Linda, for her time spent editing my manuscript.

To all the contributors in the chapter "Boons We offer the World," I say thank you for your wisdom shared.

I am forever indebted to Dr. Robert Moore for his taking me on in apprenticeship for deeper understanding of my archetypal system-self, self-realization, and encouragement to be who I am, and for also giving my heart a language of understanding.

Lastly, I am thrice blessed by the loving encouragement of my wife who stands with me in my many endeavors and zeal for living.

Contents

Introduction

"Devote yourself therefore to the journey
within, that leads to your destiny without."
—Dakota Michael Windancer

It is no surprise to me that this book was authored mostly during the dark time hours. During the deepest sleep cycles, head and heart reconcile the dynamics of emotion and reasoning into the *internal boil* waiting to be expressed.

Finding and **living your bliss** is what this book is about. When you no longer mind the inconvenience of time frames and effort, *bliss* may be the driver of your vessel.

If you have ever daydreamed, wondered, or been in awe of the unexplainable, this book has something for you.

If you have ever felt stuck, defeated, and insignificant, this book has some gifts to share with you.

This book is about creating a *revised* or *greater version* of yourself. It offers helpful tools and insights for developing a *Hero's journey* for finding *your True Self.*

One last thing, I do not wish to prop myself up as an expert on anything. My *ideas, values, attitudes,* and *beliefs* presented here have been formulated through living experience and mentoring from wiser folk than myself. Much of what I have written is based on the work and discoveries of *Dr. Robert Moore,* whose work has inspired my own self-realization and search for the greater life awaiting me. I also wish to acknowledge *Shadow Work Inc.* for their facilitation and loving container of wisdom from which I have been honored to dip my cup. I have merely answered a call to find myself and have never looked back since.

This book was written from the heart and soul of a *spiritual cheerleader*. What I invite you to do is *simmer* in the questions I have raised long enough to formulate a pathway that leads to your *bliss*. I embrace your disagreement on any points raised within this offering. In fact, disagreement, I have found, adds flavor and taste to greater dialogue and meaningful process. My greatest desire and joy would be knowing that you created a *landscape of heart for meeting yourself* on the sacred ground of *Metanoia* and *found* **A Greater Life that Awaits**. Infinite blessings on that journey!

—Dakota Michael Windancer

Creation Story and Blessing

Sometime during existence that predated the concept known today as time when reality and conceptual knowing could not be measured, there existed only the energy of *Love*.

Love in that time had no boundaries and its only ambition was to create and be creative. Emanating from this desire was born the functionality of bonding with what love had created. From this movement pairs of all types were created, pairs created in every form conceivable to the limitless power of *Love Energy*. The more that *Love* created, the more fertile *Love* became. So much to the point of *Love's* fertility, it also created *paradox* and *wonderment*. In fact, through *Love's* hidden potential sprouted everything known and understood, and even those things not understood, are *Love's* ultimate contribution to what is known today. *Love* was the giver of essence and life, form and formlessness, and movement to all things.

When time began to be measured by the wisdom brought to mankind through the creativity of *Love*, humankind began to exploit the many expressions that Love had shown to it. *Love* in its purest form was known by all living things as *THE KINGDOM*. The Kingdom was known as the meeting place where all thought, emotion, and consciousness formed an alliance in the purpose of creating *Magnetic Center*. It was the human experience of *Divine Love* and culmination. When *Love* was honored properly, humankind became *godlike*. Nothing was impossible; good and evil were integrated as a part of the whole of creation and there was no judgment. Humankind knew the plant and animal languages and was able to converse more aptly through total silence.

The *Second Beginning* started to occur when the human form begin to experiment with *Love's many expressions*. Rationality began to creep into the mind, whereas before, the heart had always led. Humankind began to reason more than feel. Reasoning had opened the door to betrayal, power lust, and the creation of mechanized warfare. Detachment began to take over the bonding instinct, which resulted in the creation of betrayal, lying, and the instinct of being greater than another. Humankind began to pervert *Love* and its fullest expression by labeling it as gooey and weak. Humankind turned to detachment and distraction as the cure for their power lust and unfulfilled desires. Humankind made the unconscious choice to externally alchemize the internal essence that was their greatest inheritance. They became wise in their mind as to disregard the expression of *Love's Balance of Opposites*.

Creativity began to manifest in war making, and love-making became inauthentic. Desires of every kind began to rule the minds of humanity, giving in to every sense object, every thought that decreased universality but propagated individuality and selfish concern. Humanity had indeed known how to live supernaturally but had decided to improve upon perfection. This resulted in the polarization of relationships of humanity to nature, humanity to animals, the oceans, rivers, and streams, and the Father Sky. Humankind had made the ultimate enemy of itself. Despite great material achievements, humanity traded compassion for a seven-mile bridge spanning a poisoned ocean. *Neglecting* the *Love* that had created him, humanity built great destructive war machines to kill from a distance so far that remorse and empathy became obsolete.

Love was, however, wise enough to *create* for the sake of Magnetic Center. Artists, poets, musicians, thespians, and the like provided the temporal joys and laughter for humankind in the hope that they would remember the inheritance that was who they once were. This means becoming the resurrection of generative life once again, instead of feeding from the *Corpse of the World* that only *they* had created.

Humankind learned too late that immortality had fled in every moment they had wasted on living off the *Corpse of the World*. The glory of humanity now and forever is in their knowing that death brings new life and that life resolves into death. Glory is fulfilled with how each individual gives to the world before leaving it. It is not, after all, what we take from the world, but what we leave to it. Wisdom teaches us that when we become old, our joy is made complete through the giving of our gifts. It is wiser still not to give them to those who do not know they are needed.

The ultimate truth of mankind is that we are Love; therefore, we have never been born, nor will we ever die, because we have always existed from the time of no time, from that universal and cosmic force that is the ultimate expression, the ultimate source, and the ultimate movement—*LOVE.*

Creation Story

The inspiration for writing this book came from the suffering of living a false narrative, and the joy of recreating a new one. Severing unhealthy soul ties to those things which held me back from living my personal *Creation Story* of authenticity was part of my *Rite of Passage* into manhood and wholeness.

Asking the right questions is the beginning of a never-ending adventure of self-discovery and reclaiming of the *Royalty within.* Contained throughout these pages are the *attitudes, values,* and *beliefs* of men and women much wiser than me, from whom I have gained strength and inspiration. I have stood on their shoulders to see farther and built a foundation where they have excavated.

The intent and purpose of this offering is to encourage and supply some helpful insights for changing, shifting, and recreating for yourself a *higher vision* of living, thus a happier destiny. I do not ask you to agree with me on anything contained within these pages, only that you *entertain* the questions long enough to see if they resonate in some way. Self-actualization can occur in as many different forms as there are people. I want to humbly affirm and cheer you on along your way. This book is my way of "standing with you" during some *dark nights of soul* that may be occurring and rooting for you in your personal breakthroughs and *summitting experiences*. My sincerest hope is that by reading these pages you are encouraged to find the strength and inspiration to be more than you think you are and discover your *treasure within* that pays the tolls on your spiritual journey of being who you are with no apologies, living out loud your profound truth, and creating meaningful connection to the world that surrounds all of us.

If one sentence within these pages sparked or illuminated a personal excavation of finding out more about yourself, then writing this has been worth the effort, and my joy greatly increased.

Blessing

May your journey through life be blessed with abundance for everything needed, constant diminishing of everything unwanted, and to see clearly through the eyes of your heart the pathway that leads you to a greater life, and the world's hopeful expectation! Love yourself whole.
—Dakota Michael Windancer

Starving to Know Who "WE" Are

"We're so engaged in doing things to achieve
purposes of outer value that we forget the
inner value. The rapture that is associated
with being alive is what it is all about."

—Joseph Campbell

I've been told by many who I am. One example of being
finalized is with the concept of being born into the sinful
nature, but out of divine image. That concept seems like a
dichotomy to me. I'm not going to debate whether it's true
or not. It could be. *My questions are how does knowing that
help me to evolve? Also, what exactly is the sinful nature or the
divine nature? Is this also a static reality that I have no hope of*

changing? What are the regulators of this nature that I could make liaison with? Didn't God make both?

We do the things we do for many reasons: parental influence, cultural acceptance, personal motives, and vocational calling. Many more can be listed. But beyond that is the *archetypal hardwiring* of our psyche that *inflates* and *cools, rises* and *falls,* like the tides of the ocean, influencing us through ever-changing *energy* levels within us. These are *real,* and they don't always have our best interests in mind, but we can work side by side with them and enlist them as allies.

Understanding what the term *archetype* means in the lexicon of psychological theory and behavior will enable us to gain greater understanding as to *who we truly are* and *why* we do the things we do.

In this chapter, with great clarity, you will understand the term *archetype* and your *archetypal hardwiring.* You will learn some strategies and processes of how to integrate these energies when needed and how to work with them. You will gain a greater understanding that you are more than what you eat, more than what you think, and more than what you feel. You will come to realize if you don't already, that you are ENERGY. Have you ever wondered what is left of you after having removed everything physical? ENERGY. *If all it takes to keep a body alive is nourishment and water, then why can't we revive a corpse with food and water?*

Archetypal energy is the dominant force within us that has much to say about our choice making, and emotional maturity. Our friend the *shadow* is involved as well, but first let us define these amazing *archetypes* that have partnership in defining us as human beings.

Let me preface that what I am about to share is that although the context of my writing may invoke a *masculine* quality, the same dominant energies I am about to speak of reside in the *female* gender as well. The reader should understand the *female* counterpart is the equal to the *masculine* term implied.

In his book *King Warrior Magician Lover*, Dr. Robert Moore explains and helps us rediscover the *archetypes* of the mature masculine known as the King *Warrior Magician* and *Lover*.

Archetypal structures within each of us serve as conduits for great charges of primal psychological energy. These are the equivalent to the instincts of other animals. They are the bedrock structures that define the human psyche's own nature regardless of the culture in which individuals live. In this sense, *archetypes* represent transpersonal, human psychological characteristics. Universal mythic characteristics such as the *hero*, *sage*, and *ruler* are fundamental *motifs* within the human psyche known energetically as *archetypes*.

Perhaps you are familiar with the saying, **"It's good to be king."** What is implied is that as the king, we become the *alpha*, the authority that passes judgement, the supreme lawmaker and giver. Also, we hold the vision to foster, affect, and nurture those whom we are responsible for. The *King, in his fullness*, is at the center of every situation and constellates that center on behalf of his domain. The *King, in his fullness*, inspires his subjects through bestowing riches, blessing, and generativity. The desire to be co-creator of a better world, envisioning improved health, prosperity, and happiness is the manifestation of *King energy in its fullness*.

Joy is the *gateway energy* of the King. When you are in a joyful state, you are accessing your *King* energy. A true *king* takes great delight in seeing those around him flourish. Jesus the Christ is the greatest example of *King* energy manifest.

Remember I said earlier that our friend the *shadow* gets involved with these energies? *The Shadow King* manifests as tyrannical or as a weakling. Caligula of ancient Rome is a good example of a *Shadow King,* or in his case, emperor. Caligula, Pol Pot, Kim Jong-il, Joseph Stalin, and Adolf Hitler were effective leaders. However, their brutality toward their own people and the world at large is the legacy they left behind as *Shadow Kings,* with the obsession of power being more important than the betterment of their people. Absolute power corrupts absolutely is the embodiment of the *Shadow King.*

Warrior Energy in its fullness is mission oriented. That mission is in submission to authority put over him and acts as guardian, protector, and servant on behalf of the people. The true *warrior* fights to preserve life rather than to take it. Good *Warrior Energy* is invested in changing what needs to be changed and severing any ties with what is not needed. *Warriors* see things as dualistic. They are expert tacticians and differentiate between fact and fiction and allow their lenses to identify what and who the true enemies are.

Mohandas Gandhi embodied *Warrior Energy* in its fullest positive expression. Without firing a shot, Gandhi defeated the entire British empire through the warfare of pacification. As an *expert tactician,* Gandhi understood that conventional warfare would result in bloodshed and thousands of deaths for his people. Waging war through unconventional means brought independence to his nation and peace, at least for a time, between Hindus and Muslims. The true *warrior* finds a way to complete the mission with minimal loss of life.

Shadow Warriors fight for glory and medals. In the movie *Patton*, there is a scene that exemplifies Patton's *Shadow Warrior* tendency. In this scene, his men are marching to the next battle exhausted, hungry, and demoralized. Patton drives by on a jeep and one of his men says, **"There goes old blood and guts."** Another soldier replies, **"Yeah, our blood, his guts."** Further along in the movie, Patton is known to have said to Omar Bradley, while looking out over the carnage of dead corpses and debris, ***"God, I do love it so!"***

General Custer won acclaim for himself during the Civil War for his bravery and recklessness, at a time when the North desperately needed a leader. During the Indian wars at the Battle of the Greasy Grass, known as the Little Bighorn, Custer divided his men and was greatly outnumbered by the Lakota, Cheyenne, and Arapaho tribes, resulting in a massacre for the Seventh Calvary regiment of the United States Army. It is still being argued today whether it was a *tactical error* or Custer's *inflated* sense of egotism that caused their demise. Either way, his *Shadow* created that end.

"Shoot them all and let God sort them out" is the mantra of a *Shadow Warrior*. In his book, Robert Moore speaks of two kinds of cruelty, *cruelty without passion*—obeying orders, and *cruelty with passion*—vengeful and bloodlust.

An example of the first kind is a practice the Nazis used in training the SS Officer Corps. Candidates would raise puppies, caring for them in every way, feeding, grooming, and creating a relationship with them. Then at a time prescribed by their superiors, candidates were ordered to kill their puppies with no sign of feeling. You can now understand how that kind of training produced the extermination of millions of Jews. Unbelievable to us, those same men believed they were the "good guys."

The second kind of cruelty is the example of the Turkish army in World War I. After taking an Arab village, the soldiers delighted in cutting open pregnant women with their bayonets, ripping out their unborn babies and hanging them around their necks.

With these examples given, you can discern for yourself that *Warrior Energy* is capable of both atrocity or positive affecting. Gandhi's approach toward an enemy, or this last example, is the manner of integration.

The world of the *Magician* is comprised of *thought* and *reflection*. It is not only the *archetype* of awareness and of insight but also knowledge of anything that is not immediately apparent or commonsensical. It is the *archetype* that governs what is called in psychology, *"the observing ego."* The *Magician archetype*, in concert with the observing ego, keeps us insulated from the overwhelming power of the other archetypes. It is the mathematician and the engineer in each of us that regulates the life functions of the psyche. The fullness of *Magician Energy* shows up through doctors, lawyers, priests, CEOs, plumbers, electricians, research scientists, psychologists, and many others when they are working to turn raw power to the advantage of others. Witch doctors and shamans, with their rattles, amulets, herbs, and incantations, are accessing their internal *Magician* and so are the research technicians who are looking for cures for our most deadly diseases. The *true Magician*, with his fullest human vessel, aims at fullness of being for all things through the compassionate application of knowledge and technology.

The *Shadow Magicians* are responsible for producing the death camps of World War II and the doomsday weapon that today looms over our heads.

Geo engineering is the mastery over nature and propaganda ministries of the press and government. The *proper function* of the *Magician* is being perverted into controlled press briefings, censored news, and artificially orchestrated political rallies. *Shadow Magician* shows up as *Manipulator*. The *Manipulator* maneuvers people by withholding from them information they may need for their own well-being. Commanding exorbitant fees, the *Manipulator* gives just enough information to demonstrate his superiority and great learning. *The Shadow Magician* is not only detached but cruel. Legal professions have access to hidden knowledge that can make or break us. After they charge an outrageous fee for their service, we may or may not benefit from their service. Whenever we become detached, unrelated, and withholding what we know could help others or use our knowledge as a weapon to demean and control others, in bolstering our own status and wealth, we are doing the *Shadow Dance of the Magician. Manipulator*, therefore, can be framed as the *active* pole of the *Shadow Magician*.

The *passive pole* of the *Shadow Magician* shows up through naivety or being the "*Innocent One.*" This is the individual who doesn't want to know themselves and does not want to put in the earnest effort required to becoming skilled at containing and channeling power in constructive ways. This individual does not want to take the responsibility that belongs to the *true Magician*. He does not want to share and teach. He does not want the task of helping others in the necessary step-by-step way of proper initiation. He wants to learn just enough to derail those who are making worthwhile efforts. He protests the innocence of his hidden power motives and is too good to make any real efforts himself, blocking others and seeking their downfall. *Are you able to recognize this anywhere on today's world stage?*

Lastly, the *Shadow Magician* parries any attempt to confront them, keeping us off balance by seducing us into an endless process of questioning our own intuitions about their behavior. If we challenge their innocence, they will often react with a *show of tear-jerking bewilderment* and leave us to stew in our own juices.

Thomas Jefferson, author of the Declaration of Independence, demonstrated his *Magician* qualities through his writing skills and later as president of the United States, by expanding the territory through the funded exploration of Lewis and Clark. Inventing the process of pasteurization, Louis Pasteur accessed the *fullness of Magician Energy* by working late nights in the lab with relentless study to find the process by which pathogenic bacteria is killed, reducing the transmission of diseases such as typhoid fever, tuberculosis, scarlet fever, polio, and dysentery.

In my conclusion of *Magician Energy*, I must mention that the *true Magician* knows how to create and enter sacred space. Ministers who show up only to deliver a sermon on Sunday will not hold the proper energies for transformational experience on behalf of their congregation, nor will they be able to provide the pathway to alchemy for those during counselling who need that transformational experience. There is much to say about the *container of sacred space*, its creation and intention. However, that is another chapter to which I will devote the proper and necessary attention that is deserved.

What kind of person would I be without the archetype of the Lover? Let me give you a perspective. Accessing the *King* without a *Lover*, I would be a self-entitled tyrant in ruthless command, or a weakling, abdicating my power to others. Without access to the *Lover archetype*, *Magician Energy* could show up as a *detached manipulator* or *naïve innocent one*, always planning but never doing and working to undermine the efforts of others. My *Warrior Energy* most likely would inflate to either a sadistic or masochistic expression of *"woe is me"* or the *pleasure of witnessing the suffering of others.* If I were fortunate enough to have been raised by perfect parenting, there is a chance that I would have the ability to constellate the positive poles of those *archetypal energies*. The truth is, however, that it requires great skill in learning to access and regulate them properly, so I will choose to error on the side of pragmatism.

It is the *Lover archetype* that calls me from sleep and put into words the thoughts of my heart and creative boil in pursuit of my bliss. The *archetype* of the *Lover* is always creating and energizing. In its *fullness, Lover Energy* is sensitive and leads to compassion and empathy for all things. *The Lover* sees union in everything bound together in mysterious ways. He sees, as they say, the world in a grain of sand. Color, art, languages, even highly abstract thoughts like theology, philosophy, and science are felt through the senses. The man who is deeply in touch with *Lover Energy can read people like a book.* He is excruciatingly sensitive to their shifts in mood and can *feel* their hidden motives. In his capacity to feel at one with others and with the world, he must also *feel their pain.* Others may be able to avoid pain, but the man in touch with the *Lover* must endure it. Artists and psychics manifest *Lover Energy* most clearly. The world of sight and sounds, aromas, the thinking with his heart and head, is the realm of *Lover Energy.* When we stop to smell the roses and *simply feel* with no pressure to perform, we are accessing the *Lover.* When we *intuit* or have *hunches* about situations occurring in our lives, we are experiencing the *Lover. Lover Energy,* furthermore, does not yield well to boundaries, which brings us next to the *shadow poles* of *Lover Energy.*

Possessed by the Shadow Lover, the energy works toward the destruction of those held by it and to the destruction of those around him.

The active pole of the *addicted Lover* is to ask themselves the question, *"Why should I put any limits on my sensual and sexual experience of a vast world that holds unending pleasures for me?"* The *Shadow Lover* as *Addict* becomes lost in an ocean of his senses. Sunsets and reverie are not his only seducer. By getting drawn into the loneliness of a train whistle at night or the emotional devastation of a fight at the office, the *Addicted Lover* becomes a victim of his own sensitivity. Knowing there is no money to spare, the *Addicted Lover* will spend grocery money meant for family at the race track. Being warned of the early signs of cirrhosis of the liver, the *Addicted Lover* continues to drink himself to an early death. Living for the moment, the Addicted *Lover* is in constant search of the *Cosmic Orgasm* that does not exist. Boundaries are the way out for the *Addicted Lover*, but instead, he will look for his spirituality in the euphoria of *instant gratification.*

The passive pole of the *Impotent Lover* is a life of chronic depression. They feel a lack of connection to everything. If you ask them at this moment, *"What are you feeling?"* they most likely will answer, *"I don't know."* The *Impotent Lover* will fall into self-loathing and have no true sense of themselves. They can feel that there is nothing to live for and lack any vision for their lives. Without the imaging or visioning of the *Lover*, people often perish. *Widows* and *widowers* are prime examples of how this energy inflates after the loss of a significant other and often results in depression and the lack of any vision for continued living. I am sad to say that I am well acquainted with the truth of that, by witnessing the dynamics of *Impotent Lover* after my mother buried my dad.

We have discussed and given examples of the basic energetic hardwiring of the human psyche. You now have a good understanding of how the *King, Warrior, Magician,* and *Lover* aspects manifest themselves into our living experiences. We must respect the fact that these energies are real and not a psychological fairytale. Integration and working with these energies, now that we can recognize and identify them, will empower us as individuals to act out of the fullness of the *archetypes* rather than *reacting* from the inflation of their emotional charge.

The greatest power or force known to mankind is love. Love can conquer the human heart. It is within the human heart that most ills of society emanate. Learning to be better *Lovers* will build a better world, a world of collective empathy, compassion, sensitivity, and co-creation. As better *Lovers*, creative life forces will seep from our pores and foster the act of once again becoming our *brothers' keepers. How do we become better Lovers?* We do this by using mindfulness in creating boundaries for our sensual and sexual appetites. Making love and excess eating will not rid ourselves of a lonely heart but connecting in genuine ways to others will. Supporting others in their dreams and goals is a wonderful way to show empathy and love toward those reaching for the stars. Taking up a musical instrument can be a study of meditative mindfulness. It is like connecting your heart to your head, no matter your level of proficiency. Walking in nature and allowing your eyes to not only take in the trees but what the space between the branches and leaves look like is a form of *Lover Energy.* Cloud gazing and looking for images, imagining them as more than clouds even to the point of renaming them is a form of love. I refer to the clouds as *sky barges.* The study of a new language increases your capacity to connect more deeply to a culture unfamiliar to you. Lastly, allowing excess into your living experience can remind you that the result and antithesis of inflated *Lover Energy* is *boundaries. It may not be what you want, but it is what you need!* These are a few of the infinite variety of choices to access your *Lover*. Have fun; invent. Be insanely silly. *The Lover* is about being playful and playing in the playground provided to us. You will always get what you need, even when you are not sure what it is you want. I promise that is true!

With the advent of the internet and the many uses of cyber space, we have accessed the *Magician*, but not always for the betterment of the world. Being better at integrating *Magician Energy*, you must learn to use detachment as a tool to see what exactly is in front of you. *Magician Energy* calls you to *"step back"* from a problem so that you may see the many *options* available for solving it. The *archetype* of the *Magician* asks me to sit in the question long enough for the answer to emerge, allowing my *inner Sage* to speak from intuitively knowing what my brain is still struggling to sort out. *The voice of wisdom is often heard in the deafening roar of silent reflection.* It is within the silent recesses of mindful reflection that my introvert can dialogue with the *radiant King* that shapes my vision of living that sustains me.

It is within this same container that meaningful dialogue is held with my *Warrior* to know the *"how"* and *"what"* that will be required for me to manifest that vision. My *Warrior* will supply the needed logistics, plan of execution, and resolve in accomplishing my goal. My *Lover* will unify with the *archetypes* to provide the creative flow and variety of mediums to shape, paint, give texture and color to that envisioning. Without the *sacred space* of the *Magician*, I can expect no magic to occur. As with the other *archetypes*, I must give and allow a voice for my *Magician* to speak. *Alchemy* occurs through the magic of *Magician Energy*. I learn through magic that fear serves me through giving respect and reverence to those entities that threaten me. It is through this knowing that my fears are *alchemized* into finding the courage of my *Warrior* who wishes to speak, saying, *"I was designed to do wonderful things and I shall do them."*

Dialogue between men and women at times can be downright comical. John Gray said, **"Men are from Mars, women are from Venus."**

Many men will relate to this statement, *"It's not that I don't like having conversations with women, it's that it takes too long."* And I believe many women will identify with these statements as well, *"It's no surprise to me that he won't ask for directions. He doesn't listen to me when I speak either."*

The dynamic occurring in this common theme between men and women is that *Warrior Energy* is meeting *Lover Energy* and they are *diametrically* opposed to one another. A mentor of mine explained to me that in conversation, men report and women rapport. Men are more invested in data that is *Warrior* based. Women, on the other hand, and not the rule, tend toward connecting, which is *Lover* based. Do you see the problem? *It's like trying to bobsled on asphalt!*

Warrior wants to move. It is about action not speech. It is about facts, not a story. It is about cutting to the chase and accomplishing, not *admiring the magnificent sunset along the way!*

There are always exceptions to the rule, but most men are hardwired with more *Warrior Energy* than women. Men can seem impatient because their *Warrior Energy* comes on line so easily, and when *Warrior Energy inflates*, it's not the time for long conversations. *Regulation* needs to occur before that can happen.

Warrior is invested in doing whatever it takes in completing his mission. It is the *Warrior* that will exhaust himself to the point of expiration or divorce in trying to provide the extras for his beloved. It is the *Warrior* that stays up all night protecting those he loves. He will study his enemies meticulously for finding the plan for their defeat. It is the *Warrior* who serves out of sense of duty, either to King, Queen, or President. It is the noble *Warrior* that fights to preserve life and extinguishes life with reverent reserve. The *true Warrior* will fight for justice, never taking life without cause. His battle cry is, "It is a good day to die!"

Sovereign Energy up until now has been referred to as *"King."* Out of respect for sisters, mothers, and grandmothers I shall refer to King Energy as *"Royal or Sovereign."* *Did you just see what happened?* I accessed my *Magician* to revise a term used throughout this chapter and reframed through words, *Royal* or Sovereign, as a replacement for *King.* I accessed my *Lover* to be more inclusive on behalf of the female gender in using more gender-neutral terms for creating better connection to them. Lastly, I accessed the *Sovereign Energy* to foster the goodwill of both genders by seeing the bigger picture of serving ALL.

Royal Energy is about the bigger picture. It's how to foster, affect, and nurture through blessings and riches the betterment of the entire community. *Royal Energy* is concerned with governing wisely and justly.

Royal Energy in its fullest expression allows those around him to shine. *Royal Energy* takes great delight in witnessing the emergence of an individual's star rising.

Five aspects of blessing are the domain of Royal Energy. They are (1) active commitment in helping another to manifest their dreams, (2) recognizing others for their achievements, (3) meaningful touch, (4) spoken blessing, and (5) attaching a high value on another picturing a special future. Remaining calm during the storm, others take their cue from the Royal example. *"Acting the part,"* Royalty affect themselves into becoming whatever is needed for the situation. Always looking up, the *true Royal* knows that they answer to a power greater than themselves. *King* David of Israel sent Uriah, the Hittite, to his death by putting him in the front of battle where it was fiercest. As *King*, he could take his widow into his chambers and father a child through her. His motive was her beauty; *Shadow Lover Energy* moved through carnal desire and *Shadow King*, absolute power!

After Nathan, the prophet, revealed David's transgressions to him, David repented before the God of Israel and could maintain his Kingdom even after that mighty scandal.

Humility is the cloak worn by the possessor of the *Royal Energy* for he knows that through future generations his legacy, good or bad, will be remembered and chronicled by historians.

Lastly, the *Royal* person is centered. He incorporates the *sacred* in the *profane*, the *infinite* in the *finite*, the *potential* into the *actual*, and the *unconscious* in the *conscious*. *Royal* as procreator inspires subjects by beholding them and dispensing riches to them. As *Transforming vessel*, he distributes a concentration of power to the created world.

As structurer, he encourages education, translates divine order into technology, theology, and philosophy. He upholds divine order through human law and fortifies against inner and outer enemies, chaos, and death.

We now have healthy and sound understanding of what *archetypal energy* is and defined the abstraction of the word *archetype*. We have come to know that our psychic internal hardwiring is composed of the *Shadow*, *Royal*, *Magician*, *Warrior*, and *Lover* qualities. There are more, but I am speaking only of the hardwiring. We are composed also of ego, consciousness, and the unconsciousness things we don't know about which relates to our *shadow self* as well. We have learned how to access these qualities and have an idea of how to properly integrate their power. Examples have been given through the lives of others to provide proof of the effectiveness of these energies both in *shadow* form and in their fullest and *golden* expression.

To provide you with a very simple and practical way of working with these newfound aspects of who we are, I invite you to take notice of everyday living in terms of these various energies. When grocery shopping, if you find yourself reading labels and figuring budget before the checkout, ask yourself, *"What quadrant of my archetypal energy am I accessing?"*

"Is it the *Magician, Warrior, Lover* or *King*?"

"*Is it all of them?*" If you are watching television and a commercial is appealing to your sense of entitlement, *what archetype is that appealing to?* One last example, if your senses are being *manipulated by* color, sound, and taste, what *archetype* is being accessed by that commercial sales pitch?

Practicing the recognition of what archetypes are being accessed during commercials is a way for you to become more aware or conscious of them in your everyday interaction among the human family. If you witness anger, you know that the *Warrior* is on line. How you *deal* with anger is your *shadow* or your *gold*. If you feel a need to create space between you and another, you are accessing the *Magician* that needs to step back and provide options for your interaction. When you stop your car to allow a person to cross in front of you, even though you are in a hurry, you have *yielded* yourself to them out of your *Lover quadrant*. Dr. Robert Moore is credited with having discovered these energies that exist in every culture on this planet. I would invite you to google his name for further study and access to his perspectives on this subject. He devoted his entire life to bettering mankind by teaching about *who we are* with this paradigm. I have provided a mere glimpse. In no way is this a comprehensive study, but merely an overlay into a larger vault of microcosmic knowing. Entire books have been written for each archetype and there is a fascinating wealth of inspiring knowledge to be gained by further study into *who we are* in relation to *archetypal hardwiring*.

In conclusion, what we can hope to gain by utilizing this special knowledge is self-mastery. Carl Jung refers to it as "*Individuation*," which is a completely natural process of transformation whereby the personal and collective unconsciousness are brought into consciousness by means of *dreams*, *active imagination*, and *free association* to be assimilated into the whole personality. *Wholeness* therefore is the equal integration of the *archetypes* and *shadow*. This is a way to incarnate the Kingdom of God and to live as a "*Twin of Christ.*"

Do I wish to be only the god of war, living out of that energy alone, or do I wish to elevate myself to living as a twin of Christ by integrating them all?

Shakespeare said that we are actors on this stage of life, and that in their time men and women play many parts. *What if we could consciously integrate the best of what we admire in men and women and be that as an individual? If we were willing to work on ourselves to that end, would we not be co-creating a vibrant, generative, and positive world? If we don't start now, then when?*

Friends, it is time for us to use the knowledge our modern sages have given us. Remember, "We see the world not as it is, but the way we are." Might it be true that it is WE, who need a bit of transformation and not so much the world? *Wouldn't it be nice to turn on the television and see men and women honoring one another for their various gifts and talents rather than witnessing the insulting and minimizing agents that has become the norm?*

Gandhi said, **"We must be the change we wish the world to be."** He was that, and he did! *Are we to be any* *less?* Even with minimal effort, the least we can expect is a shift of consciousness to occur. Do that daily and we are changing our reality and perception, and gradually we are changing the world!

Living from *apotheosis*, or as uninspired servant to emotion and senses, seems to be the choice we are facing daily.

"The master in the art of living makes little distinction between his work and his play, his labor and his leisure, his mind and his body, his education and his recreation, his love and his religion.

"He hardly knows which is which. He simply pursues his vision of excellence in whatever he does, leaving others to decide whether he is working or playing. To him, he is doing both." (Anonymous)

Our Perception of Reality

The ancient Talmud states this, **"We see the world not as it is, but the way we are."** The question that surfaced within me after pondering that axiom is, *"What is the way that I am and how did that develop?"*

We are now living in perhaps one of the most divisive and irrational periods of current history. While there does exist a true *"androgyny,"* known in First Nation communities as a *Two Spirit* (a person who is simultaneously feminine and masculine, although not necessarily in equal parts) within the human family, the gap between the authentic and the envisaged, or conceptualized, is ever widened by individual viewpoint. *Gender identification* is a hotly contested political issue. Biology and physiology no longer define male or female, but through the fickleness of individual feelings, we are being forced to reframe how we define gender in modern society almost to the point of questioning one's own. There is widespread polarity in governmental decision-making and leadership. *The "left" is right and the "right" is wrong.* Dualism seems to be the *reigning spirit* ruling mankind's reasoning. We argue over everything and agree on little. Being the *Alpha* in the shining light has become more important than *"standing with"* and being a part of a united effort for positive affecting. Reality, therefore, is as flexible for some as the imagination will allow.

Maybe you have similar frustrations with knowing where and how to stand amongst the complexities of relational living.

My worldview and yours is shaped by the *way we are.* *"What is the way I am?"* is the question that inspires me to write about our collective perceptions of reality and the desire of creating a world of infinite blessing energies by living relative truth, and mastering life.

How apropos it is that I, as a man among men, am in the *"middle age"* of my living experience answering the question of *"who am I"*? *What is my approach in my personal middle age crusade?* Akin to the Knights Templar, I am compelled to search for the holy grail of my reality. I must reconcile that I am empowered in *finding my bliss and transcendent grace,* for positive impact on the world around me.

This chapter will reveal to you (1) defining how perception affects reality, (2) how to change or shift one's own reality, and (3) mindful management of our perception of reality.

Wikipedia defines *reality* as the state of things as they exist, rather than as they may appear or might be imagined. *Reality* includes everything that is and has been, whether it is observable or comprehensible. A still broader definition includes that which has existed, exists, or will exist. It seems by this definition that we traverse *reality* in both the abstract and concrete world of experience and thought.

Perception is defined as the ability to see, hear, or become aware of something through the senses or a way of regarding, understanding, or interpreting something such as a mental impression.

How does perception affect our reality? How is perception formulated? How can I know that my perception is accurate?

Belief systems are a component of *perception. Confirmation of bias* is a concept that states if value is placed in something, then indeed it holds value, whether it does for you or not. My belief that it does, has been pre-determined, so my *perception* has given value to something through my bias. My belief constructs my *perception,* which in turn shapes my *reality* in placing value upon something.

Alcoholism shaped my *reality* for many years. Being discovered by who is now my wife, I was practicing dry firing my 9mm pointed to my head to get used to the sound in preparation for ending my then miserable existence. In periods of distress or desperation, vulnerability seems to supply the *magic* needed for a *reality shift.* My wife valued me. She pulled the gun away from my head and poured herself into my soul by crying and asking me why it was that I could not see in myself the many talents and treasures that were so clearly seen by her. I had been given a reprieve from a tragic ending, yet in my *skewed perception*, she shone too bright for me and I felt even more shame, guilt, and desperation because I was too unlike her. My *jaundiced perception* had now placed *transference* upon her into the *"Golden Goddess"* that I would never be worthy of. In this state of mind, I think it is safe to say that my *perception* was formulated out of my sense of shame, guilt, remorse, and worthlessness almost resulting in my final arrival (death). I am happy to report that I lived to know without a *shadow* of doubt that my perception of reality and who I was, was not accurate. The same holds true even today, but for opposite reasons.

What was needed for me was a *new beginning*, a do-over of sorts, *but how?* It was clear that my *reality* needed a *reformulation*. I reasoned that I must create a mythology for myself that I could believe in and embrace 100 percent. During this search for a new beginning, I realized that the wounds carried into adult life from childhood had much to do with my perception of self, family, friends, and the world in general. Whatever was about to happen before, during, and after this *re-creation event* needed to be an epic shift of perception for me or I was facing exile into a world of chaotic drunken revelry, looking for a *cosmic orgasm that does not exist,* winding up dead or in jail.

Manipulating my reality was the answer to my dilemma. Sobriety was a logical start for a happier reality, *but would that sustain me? What about the deep wounds of my soul and spirit? The betrayals perpetrated onto me by the sovereign figures of my youth? What would be the process that would become my breakthrough into entering a reality of peace, joy, and sovereignty of spiritual knowing?*

It's been said that when the apprentice is ready to learn, the *Merlin figure* appears.

For the first time in too long a period, I put a strong intent of *mindfulness* into how and exactly what action I would take to become the person who I was designed to be. Planning, preparing, securing mentorship and safety were the first stepping stones to embarking on the *mythological hero's journey* that I had intuitively felt. Immediately after making that decision to do whatever it takes to change, my perception and reality began to shift from one of despair to one of hope, anticipation, and magical yearning. I had no guarantee for positive outcome, yet I had nothing to lose. There seems to be a *liminal reality* that emerges, like Cortes ordering his men to burn the ships after landing in

Veracruz, it only allows the options *of victory or death.* In the same way, my *mindfulness* of managing reality would either lead me to the home of connecting heart and head, reconciling my *shadow* behaviors, or I would die in the misery I had become familiar with. Complexities are often solved through simplicity.

It was the week of Easter 1999 that I went to the Gila Wilderness of New Mexico to die. Answering the call of my spirit to a *Vision Quest,* my *intention* was to put to death the immature boy, so that the mature man could be born. It was during the *ceremony/ritual* known as the Native American *Vision Quest* that *I died* and was *reborn, recreated* with a *new heart,* a *new name,* a *new vision for living.* Fasting four days and four nights changes your consciousness and allows the *medicine* of the Earth Mother to dialogue intimately with you through color, sound, and silence. Perception is changed immensely when your belly is empty. Ritual becomes the benediction of both day and night. One becomes grateful for what was taken for granted. *Deprivation is the blessing of excess* and *everything is upside down, turned around,* and *within the chaos of not knowing, the outcome is the pure pleasure of first-time eyes to see the unseen and first-time ears to hear the call of the Raven* and *the wonderment of nature* in *general.* Deprivation allows the eyes to see the shimmer in the channels of the *river as a chorus of dancing lines, each taking their turn to bow and recede. I correlated what I saw with my eyes to the dance I wanted to make my life emulate: shining, bowing, receding, and progressing as the flowing of a river.* Intuition is amplified to the degree of feeling the spin of the earth beneath where you are sitting. Emotions float to the top of your consciousness and the *new lens* of seeing reveals the *cause* and the *cure* for any ailment. *Transcendence* comes in forms that seem like fictitious conjuring, yet you are a *living witness* and *participant* in the *cosmic melodrama*.

Whatever the term one chooses to refer to it, *Magic, Transcendence, God, The All,* the list could on go *ad infinitum*; "IT" is *always* available. "IT" *always* has been, and *always* will be. That to me is a part of reality that cannot be seen but only experienced. Only when the willingness to surrender to the *unknown* becomes more intentional than hanging on to my finite understanding am I able to experience the *unseen reality*. There are many more pages that could be shared about this *one* of many amazing experiences with non-ordinary reality, but by now you get a clear picture and evidence that perception affects reality, that reality can be *manipulated* many ways. *Mindfulness* in managing our perception and reality can produce *wonderment* and *open portals* into a *non-ordinary reality* that can lead us into finding our *personal bliss. Sometimes the best way to find yourself is losing yourself to the life that is unknown, yet patiently waits.*

James Allen wrote the literary essay and book, *As a Man Thinketh.* This book deals with the power of thought and its use and application. What I am aware of, how I interpret events and the world around me and my sense of knowing makes up my *perception,* which dictates my *reality.* What I believe is true, or data available to me, is how I create the reality I live and what I value as well. First Corinthians 13:9, New Living Translation of the Holy

Bible: *"Now our knowledge is partial and incomplete, and even the gift of prophecy reveals only part of the whole picture."* Humility, I believe, is always a good component of healthy reality, and I might add, a mindful way of manipulating it. This is also a way of managing our perception of reality—keeping in mind that even what we see with our eyes is greatly affected by the *shadow* in hues of *color* and *character* that keep us from seeing vividly everything composed.

We have looked at a variety of ways in defining how perception affects reality. We have discovered and implemented ways to manipulate reality, and within the discussion, built in a way of mindfully managing our perception through *checking motives, being clear on our intention,* and *planning,* to name a few.

Doing this, we have now added an extra dividend of knowledge to accrue interest within the *temple of deeper understanding.* Receiving answers to the questions asked will allow us to ask better questions as a separate set of complexities arise. It was Albert Einstein who said, ***"It is not that I am so much smarter than anyone else, but that I am more willing to sit in the question longer than most."***

We must conclude that reality is not a fixed point. It is not stationary but *elastic.* Reality *is different for you and me sitting at the same train station at the same time.* We know this because we create our own reality through perception. Remembering parts of what make up perception are *thought, belief,* and *values.* These components come via environment, culture, education, home structure, and even our personal wounding. Knowing this, it makes sense to ask the question, *"Why would I expect you to experience reality the same way that I do?"*

"How can I do better at honoring another's reality to maintain connection?" Another question and integration of the mindfulness in managing perception of reality could be, *"Where is the meeting ground for our diverse interpretation of life as reality?"*

"What can we hold meaningful dialogue about, though we view the world through entirely different lenses?" Lastly, *"Isn't it indeed a blessing of the great mystery to have given* perception *to our psyche in such diverse generosity?"*

In *the Gnostic Gospel of* Thomas, Jesus said, **"If you give rise to that which is within you, what is within you shall save you. But if you do not give rise to that which is within you, what you do not have shall destroy you."**

These words for me are the continuous invitation to take inventory on my *internal* and *external* condition, be it spiritual, mental, or physical. In creating a happier reality, I must find the willingness to be more *self-examining*, be willing to *lose myself to not knowing for a while, by taking a hero's journey like Odysseus*, if need be, and to *prove* to myself and others that we do, indeed, have a say in our destiny. I can *alchemize* the *lead* of my life, into the *gold* of new living experiences. I do this by practicing frequently what these pages have revealed. I practice for the joy of practicing betterment, and not for the destination of arrival.

Remembering that I see the world not the way it is, but the way *I* am. *Not* liking *how* the world looks for me is a clear indication that I have work to do. I have acquired some fine tools to assist me in that work. I can now be the change I wish the world to be and hold liaison with the whole and not just a part. Application of knowledge is wisdom. Wisdom externalized is how we become the *shakers* and *movers* and *spiritual artists* for greater worldbuilding. Let's start building together!

Dancing with Our *Shadow* Partner

Our greatest glory, monumental achievements, and creativity, leading to deeper understanding and human connection, are slumbering in the hardened clay of the human psyche known as the *Shadow*. Mining for the gold within that hardened clay is the dance, a journey of wonderment and great reward and personal realization.

There have been too many broken promises made to myself, resulting in shame and detached existence from whom I'd truly like to be. *There is a man who walks beside me that is generative, balanced, compassionate, and noble. That man is real, yet he is not a constant manifestation of living purpose.* This is among many reasons why I wanted to share and discuss the topic of the *shadow* within the human psyche. In a moment of grace and numinous inspiration, I heard a voice within me say, *"Look for me in places you would think you'd never find me."* It was that same moment I knew intuitively that I must search for my authentic soul through the *shadows* of my living. Since I have failed too many times trying to live in the light, perhaps I would do better searching in the darkness of my soul. If God created everything made, then that meant the Divine darkness as well. This made sense to me and became a logical way to activate Self-Realization.

Upon reading this chapter, you will learn: (1) what the *shadow* is, (2) how it manifests, (3) what its message is, and

(4) how to work with your *shadow* for a positive outcome to previous negative behavior.

By acknowledging the need for some change to occur, we are now accepting the invitation to our personal "*Shadow Dance.*" Here is how we begin. We will define what the *shadow* is, what it consists of, what its nature is, why it exists, what it does, and how I can, as an unskilled dancer, move without stepping on its toes. This will open the door to defining the dynamics of the dance itself. We will explore the *music, tempo,* even the *lyrics* within the definition of this clandestine dance partner, so that we will twist and turn and gracefully glide within the *Shadow's* embrace and befriend what was once our great antagonist. Lastly, as the dance nears the end, we will have discovered the powers and talents of our *Shadow Partner* and integrate them on our own behalf. We will alchemize the negative aspects of its tyrannical leading on the dance floor of life. We will teach it through our understanding of it and how to enjoy a partnership of mutual honoring. The journey is also the joy. Shall we dance?

What exactly is the *shadow*? Back in the "olden days," when I was a kid, there was a camera called a Polaroid. This camera was loaded with film that instantly spit out a picture after clicking the button. You would simply pull the picture away from the negative it was held to. The negative was dark, exposing no details, only the silhouette of the main subject. The *negative* in this sense is a good representation of our *human shadow*. The *shadow* contains the details within us that we hide, repress, deny, or simply don't know about. The *shadow* contains all the parts about us that we don't want others to know about or want them to see. It is the hidden self. Whenever we are withholding something from another, we are in a *shadow* behavior. Can any of us know for sure how many stars that fill the Universe we know about? What we don't know is a *shadow*. Alcoholics may refuse to admit powerlessness over their substance abuse. They are in the throes of a *shadow*, which is denial. Simply put, the *shadow* is the negative exposure of who we are, whereas the clear picture of the Polaroid is that part of us we wish to convey and project in life.

You may be saying to yourself that you would be better off without the *shadow* in your life, so why not get rid of it. The truth is that you can't. Getting rid of your *shadow* would be like getting rid of your skin because it's too oily or the wrong pigment! You are what you are, and part of that is contained within your *shadow*.

Now for some good news. Our *shadows* act on our behalf as a distillation device for our hypocrisy. When we can no longer tolerate the braggadocios sibling going on and on about his or her personal world conquering, the *shadow*, what we have repressed, often comes online, and calls out the family member in a less than tactful way. Has this ever happened to you, or someone you know? In this example, our *shadow* is keeping us honest with our self even though it resulted in some verbal brutality toward our sibling, deserved or not.

Shadow acts also as a *"cooling agent"* to reconcile our disdain with our repression. *Shadow* is a reservoir for what is also unconscious within us, like hidden talents, and desires of all types we may not know we have until a life event triggers the evidence of them. *Shadow Nature* is not friendly. *Shadow Nature* is dark, yet it is the key to illumination and numinous experience. In a final example of the purpose, form, and intent of the human *shadow*, I offer this: If you look directly into the sunlight, what would happen? The brightness of penetrating light would blind you. Conversely, if you were locked in a dark room with no light whatsoever, would it not yield the same result? This is the proof that without the *shadow* in our lives we would never be allowed the opportunity for balanced living or seeing. *Shadow* is needed to see clearly. Our world view would be dualistic, at best, if we could only see light and dark. Think about how truly colorless and bland perspective and world view would become for unfortunate folk. *Shadow* is indeed the silhouette of a very detailed soul.

By now, you have abundant concepts of the *shadow*, how it functions, what it is, and a good definition that hopefully is not too *"heady."* We know that the *shadow* contains a lot of untapped potentials within us. We know that the *shadow* is not friendly toward us and that it can keep us from being honest and authentic. So why not get rid of it? Remember when I said earlier that it would be like trying to get rid of your skin? We would not dare throw the baby out with the bath water, would we? Remember, balance occurs with both light and dark in integration. What are the steps and choreography one must learn to skillfully make the *shadow* our ally on the dance floor of life?

One of my favorite authors, Joseph Campbell, said this, **"Opportunities to find deeper powers within ourselves come when life seems most challenging. It is by** *going down into the abyss that we recover the treasures of life."* What better way of going down into the abyss and finding the deeper powers within ourselves than through the *Shadow Dance?* Let's begin . . .

Defining the "music": Let's say that anger is a chronic component of lifestyle. What if our anger is so frequent that even our closest friends describe us as *"intense,"* that's a nice attempt, perhaps, of buffering on our behalf. We could then differentiate that as the "music": placing it out as only one part of us, it needs addressing and astute attention. We *sing* through anger. This is part "A."

Defining the "tempo": how regular is this occurring, what happened before we became angry, what was said, what was the catalyst? Was it confusion, impatience, tiredness, or did something bad happen? We must gather as much data as possible relative to the outburst and causation of our anger behavior. This is differentiated as part "B."

Defining the "lyrics": *What is the message of anger's voice, what does it want, does it want something only from me, or someone else, am I getting something out of being angry, is it a sense of power, do I want to be heard, how is my anger serving me, how is my anger causing disservice for my life?*

Lastly, am I willing to go into the abyss and find the treasure and deeper power that my anger can also yield to me? If I am, then the discovery has already begun. What is amazing about dancing with the *shadow* in this way is that if one is not truly invested in authentic intention that will reveal itself through other *shadow* behavior such as procrastination, time constraint issues, and infinite varieties of other excuse-making. This only means that the dancer has not accepted the invitation. That's okay; he or she is just not willing to dance yet! There is no shame to be felt or cast; self-discovery takes enormous courage and personal resolve. It is not the work of a faint heart; it requires rigorous honesty and authentic spirit.

After separating parts A, B, and C, then answering all the questions I have about my dance with anger, I can see from my anger's point of view what its message is, what it wants, what I may be getting from it, and how it is causing chaos and alienation from others in my living experience. To paraphrase here, I must have a meaningful dialogue with that part of me that tends toward anger and be willing to listen with intuitive ears and eyes of my heart. I must have pure intention to discover my hidden treasure and latent potentials. Now you may be wondering, *"What about that alchemy of turning the lead into gold, or more accurately, the shadow behavior into discovering its gold to give?" Is this a hidden gift I didn't know about?*

We must understand that anger is a real emotion. It is a part of us that cannot be voted out just because we aren't handling it well. This is the sacred part of the dance that only the participant can choreograph for the ending desired. It is important to keep in mind that we may have to dance with this partner many more times to learn its diversity of *music, tempo,* and *lyrics.* Anger, like any unwanted dynamic, can have infinite expressions and ways of manifesting itself. Our job is to interview those voices and expressions to find out how it wants to be integrated. There is no quick fix, shortcut, or instant over and done. Gifts you will instantly receive; however, are the gifts of wonderment and satisfaction, exploring new civilizations within you and boldly going where you and many have never gone before—just like Captain Kirk or Captain Janeway. This gift is all yours and not to be shared with the crew of the USS *Enterprise*!

We are now very acquainted with the *Human Shadow*. We know that the music of *Shadow* shows up in unwanted behavior or emotions wanting to rule us. We have defined and tracked our *Shadow's* tempo by knowing how often this dynamic occurs and where else in our living this same dynamic shows up and the circumstances that surrounded us before our *shadow* began acting out. We now have a clear understanding, too, on the lyrics or message of our *shadow*. We have great insight into what it wants and what we have been getting out of its power over us. We can even go to the extent now of characterizing it with a color, a voice, a shape, and the part that needs changing, and that is its message.

I will offer a simple example of alchemizing the negative energy of anger into a golden nugget you can use now and forever after from my experience of having danced until the music stops.

After interviewing the voice of my anger and getting answers to the questions asked, I have determined that my anger stems from my sense of not being heard or listened to seriously by my peers. The shape of my anger is like a *jagged edged boulder*. It is *large* and *looms over me*. The **color** of my anger is *red, a bright cherry red that vibrates in me. My anger's voice is loud and insolent, overwhelming and caustic, and full of toxic* phlegm. *Anger for me now is personified and more than emotion.*

We have now interviewed the *shadow* thoroughly together and are ready to implement one of many solution phases of our mutual travelling. What has kept us hostage will soon become an ingredient for a golden re-formulation of experience, present and future, provided we decide not to snooze along the road of happy destiny!

In conclusion, let me reframe and review once again the now personified energy of the human *shadow*. Anger is not my *shadow*. *The shadow was my choice of how I gave anger its action!*

How my *shadow* showed up through my anger was in the words I spoke and the tone I used. *The message of my anger was that I wanted to be heard, not dismissed, which seemed at the time like a betrayal.*

How I alchemize the *Shadow Behavior* is the intuitive process I deem best for the outcome desired by me. In this example, I see my anger as the gateway to my *Inner Warrior Energy*. My *Inner Warrior* wants to protect the sovereignty of my inner soul's desire and external sharing from those who would minimize or not give me authentic ears to hear my truth. I can now see the power of anger as an agent for changing what needs changing. It now occurs to me that my anger, or *Internal Warrior*, needs to create boundaries to protect that sovereign land within. Seeing the *shadow* energy of anger as a *warrior* who fights on my behalf for what I hold dear and sacred now becomes an ally that I can trust and honor, not an adversary.

It's not so much the protecting and boundary-making that was shadowy in nature as much as it was the method of integration. I understand that a noble *warrior* never wants to kill, maim, or dismember just for that purpose. No, *a true Warrior* serves his mission given him through defense and tactical offense designed to accomplish the mission without taking lives, literally or metaphorically. *I now have come to realize that the shadow was not my anger. Shadow shows up out of seemingly nowhere . . . It was my aggression, impulsive response and reactive manner that started a war I did not want in the first place!* I have seen through another lens!

The paradox is that I am more empowered now to see it by looking for God in all the places I would think God could not be found. The end resolution has brought me back to the beginning. I must now look at where I've been, how I arrived, and assess how I traversed the terrain. Aggression and reactive behavior are the highly combustible fuel to start wars. Remembering what didn't work for me in the past gives me pause to formulate, out of my *Noble Warrior*, a more effective plan—a plan that may include kinder words, slower speech, and honoring where my antagonist is in his thinking or emotion. *The work is to develop a cunning, wise, and expert tactician in my Inner Warrior.* If I am so skilled as to disarm my adversary, then no blood needs to be shed and there lies a chance for amicable departure in disagreement or, better yet, agreement. As my favorite author, Joseph Campbell, would say, **"The return is seeing the radiance everywhere."**

Being and Knowing

Some twenty-five hundred years ago, Buddha stated, *"All life is suffering, the cause of suffering is ignorant desire, this desire can be destroyed, the means to this is the eight-fold path."*

Most of us have been closely in touch with the impermanence of our living. Everything changes, our healthy bodies decline, our accumulation of wealth at some point dissolves, and our peace, sometimes in an instant, is ambushed by restlessness.

*Simmering in the questions of: Is this all there is to my life: eating, working, celebrations, funerals, and looking for meaningful purpose? Do the qualities of both joy and sorrow exist as the same continuum and how exactly do I approach the belief that the privilege of a lifetime is being who I **am**? How do I define who I am? These are the questions that drive my personal excavation.*

Sharing my personal insights concerning these questions will hopefully provide you with a direction for your personal *simmering,* and for finding the answers yourself to those same questions that provide commonality, and bond us as human beings.

Defining clearly what *Being* and *Knowing* mean and your own application for each is a way to further develop and integrate a way for living your *personal bliss.* I would like also to address the term aggression that mistakenly defines the *Being* of male masculinity.

Every day is conceived in both living and dying. That is physical and scientific fact. Who you were yesterday is not who you are today and is not who you will be tomorrow. In the moment I take to write these words, millions of my skin cells are dying yet being replenished with new ones, and so are yours. We are living the paradox of death and life at the same time. We celebrate the birth of our sons or daughters one day; in the next, we memorialize someone passed. Is our Being the same or has it changed somehow?

Being is defined as "the nature or essence of a person." This definition is a broad stroke, don't you think? The nature and essence of a person contains many pieces and parts we ourselves are not aware of. Parts we hide, repress, and deny called the *shadow*. We humans are complicated creatures physically and psychically. We are composed of ego, super ego, and many autonomous complexes that formulated while we were growing up. Environment, parental guidance, education, and other factors were instruments of formulating our being. We are composed of more than what we know. That brings me to the point of the other part of the title of this chapter: Knowing.

Knowing is defined as "showing or suggesting that one has knowledge or awareness that is secret or known to only a few people." Another definition is this: "Done in full awareness or consciousness." Prophets are an example of people with esoteric and mystical knowledge. Knowing can also be the full awareness of playing a musical instrument or making a grocery list.

As you can see, these simple words that we bandy with contain more complexity than we may realize. Our personal Knowing and Being is microcosmic of the great macrocosm. We Know little of our Being; however, there are ways for development and deeper understanding of both Knowing and Being.

Have you ever *known* something without *knowing* why you *knew?* If that essence could be marketed do you think there would be a great demand? What would your life be like if you knew things that most people didn't? Would it lead to a royal fostering and affecting for all living things, or selfish personal use? Would either choice yield an amount of blessing, curse, or suffering?

Developing our Being adds to our Knowing. Accumulating knowledge adds to our Being conversely. Great men and women must have formed a wonderful partnership from their *Being* and *Knowing* for accomplishing what we have come to admire about them. A strong alliance made between *Being* and *Knowing* not only provides a definiteness of purpose for us as individuals but provides both the alchemical process and passion for manifestation of that vision and purpose.

Albert Einstein stated, **"Great spirits have always encountered violent opposition from mediocre minds."** This statement makes clear to us that we must reconcile ourselves to the knowing that we will be opposed in our brilliance. Our passion must be the driving force for its integration. We must not allow the whispers of subterfuge and ridicule to prevent us from bringing our golden expression held within to the world without. Think about men like Da Vinci, Tesla, and women like Harriet Tubman and more recently Malala Yousafzai, to name a few. How would it have served our world if they sat on their *bushel of light?* All great affecters of our planet found a way to integrate their *Being* and *Knowing.*

Precocity may have been the agent responsible for early expressions made on behalf of the world for some great men and women. I believe that *honoring the boil within you* is the conduit for living naturally your *personal bliss.* As Sri Ramakrishna stated, **"Do not seek illumination unless you seek it as a man whose hair is on fire seeks a pond."** When you or I actively pursue what truly makes us come alive and what causes us to spring out of bed in the morning, we are no longer working for a company or financial compensation. We are *living our bliss* and have found our *mission* in life. We may do well to keep in mind that greatness and goodness have been labeled foolish and superfluous by the experts. Jealousy and envy have a thunderous voice but provide no rain for the blessing. Remember this when you make the decision to become the village's or world's *fool!* St. Paul said it so well during his ministry while affecting the spreading of Christianity and being told he was a fool for following Christ: "Give this fool his boast, you then being so wise." Most of us are aware of St. Paul's zeal and passion for Christ and his effect on the early church and original Apostles.

Sir Isaac Newton's first law of motion states that **"an object at rest stays at rest and an object in motion stays in motion with the same speed and in the same direction unless acted upon by an unbalanced force."** We can argue according to Newton's law that giving motion to our *bliss* is the most important step. The law of motion is the scientific ally that aids our speed, direction, and movement. Aided by these forces we gain more advanced Knowing and Being. We are simply learning to use stronger laws against weaker laws for affecting ourselves in *living our bliss*. This is spiritual, metaphysical, physical, and mental manipulation for a desired outcome.

There is an ideology among the feminist movement that seeks to reduce the masculinity of all men by eliminating the *Warrior* archetype. More than once, I have heard this statement made by women: ***"The world would be better off without men!"*** I wish to address this statement during this chapter for the reason of *Warrior Identification*. I wish to provide some relevant data concerning the *mature masculine* and the *immature masculine* energy which, in my judgement, is causing the *dis-ease* and aggression from this faction of the feminist movement. Perhaps a restoration of Patriarchal and Matriarchal relationship could transpire from differentiating between Mature Masculine *Warrior* and Immature Masculine *Warrior* Energy. I hope so.

It would be disingenuous on my part if I said that my *Being* and *Knowing* are a fixed and static arrangement of balanced expression. Indeed, they are not. My *Being* and *Knowing* are a malleable collection of paradox. I often compare my *Being* and *Knowing* to the concept of time. Time *expands* if I'm standing in line or waiting for water to boil, and *shrinks* during the magic of a wedding day, or during delightful enterprise. Isn't it curious that from our *Being* and *Knowing*, humankind invents the concept of time and then become slaves to the measurement of . . . a clock! We measure our years by birthdays and commitments through anniversaries and it's good. What about the transpiring that is in between? What will the hyphen represent on your tombstone? The question most often asked by those who seek profundity is, "What is the meaning of life?" There can be no single answer that is the correct one since we are unique in our *Being* and *Knowing*. That is a question that requires a pilgrimage lasting throughout one's lifetime and will shapeshift many times over the journey. In the book, *Reflections on the Art of Living*, Joseph Campbell says, ***"We each must bring our own meaning to life. Life has no meaning; we must be willing to let go of the life we planned, to have the life that is waiting for us."*** Further he states, ***"When we talk about settling the world's problems, we're barking up the wrong tree. The world is perfect. It's a mess. It has always been a mess. We are not going to change it. Our job is to straighten out our own lives."***

This last sentence of Campbell's has helped to shape my approach to living and I am never left without some adventure to embark upon. This approach hails me both as Mighty Conqueror and the conquered. I say "YES" to both because that is life—the struggle for *becoming*. Eating and drinking are the respite and oasis between the uphill and downhill terrain of living. Allowing too long a stay at the oasis will result in my de-evolution and a bank account of diminishing returns concerning *Being* and *Knowing*. I can declare my arrival, but I cannot escape the arguing voice I also *feel* inside me that tells me that with every ending there is also a new beginning.

There is something called Divine Magic. For me it is *Knowing* that joy and sorrow, pain and pleasure, *shadow* and light are separate parts of the same pole. I cannot name a time when each extreme has not been interrupted by the other. They are part of the same continuum and serve by working together for the creation of balance. Let's use money as an example. Money casts its *shadow* this way: When there is an abundance of it, we tend to be happy and feel more secure. When there is scarcity, we can become worrisome, fearful, and sad. I encountered this recently while at a casino. It's fun and a joyful prospect when I win but feels like an indictment when I lose. The point is this: Why does money have power over my emotions? Either way, money in this example has had power over me on both sides of the same pole! I have found that it's not very different with success or failure. My *Being* and *Knowing* is expanded through this experience.

Mankind Project is an organization made up of men who hold a Rite of Passage weekend for stout-hearted men who wish to explore themselves in many ways. The experience is ineffable for most that submit to the direction of its profound design. One question asked during my tenure in this organization was *"Who are you?"* then after answering, the question was asked again differently: *"Who are you really?"* The nature of these questions assigns permanence to impermanence and asks the *Ego* to put a period where it does not belong. Answering this question about myself is an attempt at forcing me to make up judgments about my perceptions of my personality and consciousness. Doing that, I am *massaging* my *Ego* of *identifying* which takes me out of the *being* of *knowing*. Awareness is more important than the story. Awareness and observation take me from *Ego* into the liminal space of revelatory experience. Knowing becomes a state of *being* without frame or formula. Observation and awareness are all that is required for entering the realm of *mindfulness*. The answer to, "Who do you say I am?" would reveal much more about how others see me then I could possibly convince with my definition. I could list everything I think that I am, and still it would be reduced to *how I am seen* by others. I am a storybook of singular moments that lead to my lifetime. I am many parts of a *greater whole* yet *undiscovered. Can you see me?*

Defining oneself is a personal, daily endeavor I think. We are habitual creatures, yet the qualities of self-reflection and introversion spawn spontaneous changes and turnabouts.

Identity comes from what we *identify* with. Look around the world today and you will see ubiquitous proof of that. Defining oneself also comes from agreements you have made with yourself. The truth of identity emerges through the embodiment and congruency displayed in moment to moment living. *I am flawed perfection. I am living paradox. I am dearly loved. I am the active expression of Being* and *Knowing* and that will look different tomorrow than it does today because, in contrast to time, I will shrink or expand in each moment. Static Being indicates uninspired *joie de vivre* and *lack of vision.*

Development of *Being* and *Knowing* within the individual comes through *experience, search,* and *meditation.* I learned through martial arts that the formula of *time, tension,* and *temperature* worked very well to gain maximum results for attaining flexibility. *Temperature* came from warming up the body first. Utilizing *tension* came from stretching a muscle group and allowing adequate *time* under these conditions to transpire for reaching optimal results. This process became a habitual practice, and before too long, not only could I do a split with ease, I could also do what's called a "Chinese split." I had become so proficient at developing flexibility that my sensei asked me to start classes for him. I use this same formula with the development of my *Being* and *Knowing*. I define with a clarity a topic I wish to know more about, and I *search*. I surround myself with all the information I want and begin to *meditate* on all the material. *Meditate* means for me that I envision what I am reading. I bring as much life to the written word as I can through *active imagination*. This same approach works outdoors in nature. Take everything in visually and experientially with awe and an expectation of some spontaneous revelation. The most difficult step is the last one, and that is to allow the *experience* to unfold in its own time. *Experience is the sum of each moment's mentoring*. Experience has its own agenda and teaches often that which we did not want to learn in the first place! That is the gift that we must receive with gratitude to allow the welcoming of valuable process. If we avoid becoming static, we will develop immense capacities within our *Being* and *Knowing*. Should we allow a static strain to occur, we will expand both *Knowing* and *Being* from that as well. We have only taken a detour and not the expressway!

Our internal condition most often establishes our external expression. How we feel about ourselves is in direct correlation to how we externalize those feelings, whether positive or negative. *We integrate what we internally negotiate.* The desire to bring our very best to the world, therefore, should begin by *guarding our heart*. Taking frequent inventory of ourselves by *checking in* with our conditions of spiritual, intellectual, physical, and emotional health can be a great source for finding out why we are more impatient than usual with temporary setback, or quickly irritated by people who are driving too slowly.

Centering myself by breathing in through my nose and exhaling from my mouth in a ten-count rhythm is a way for quieting my restlessness and opens the temple door to awareness and consciousness of my internal state, *Being* and *Knowing*. If I am operating anywhere but the center, I limit my effectiveness during any operation. The formula for integrating my *bliss* in a *profane* setting is found through *acceptance*. I must accept that there will be days of majestic magnanimity shown through my efforts and days of inferior, unimpressive results. Nonetheless, I will "*Act as If*" in my pursuit of *living my bliss* until the *acting* gives way to its actualization! As thunder is heard through vibrational dissonance, eternal bliss is found through the alchemy of paradox. Integration for your *personal bliss* will require the "*Warriors*" resolve for completing what has been started, the "Magicians" formula for discovering solutions to impossibilities, the "*Lovers*" compassion and creativity by connecting everything into unified purpose, and lastly, the "Royalty" of seeing with a larger scale and scope the totality of blessing, nurturing, and fostering and constellation of a thriving world-building cause.

Integrating our *Being* and *Knowing* boils down to living our truth out loud and not allowing ourselves to be shackled by fear of man or popular opinion. One caveat to this is that we must embody our truth. It is only reasonable for others' expectations to see congruency between what we say and how we show up. Only then will "Who do you say I am?" directly reflect the truth I proclaim to live in. *Progress* and not *perfection* should be our aim.

Bliss is described as perfect happiness, great joy. "Is that possible to attain?" you might ask. My answer would be yes, with this condition: if we consider bliss recognized as *a part* of a continuum.

Living my bliss isn't predicated on being perfectly happy or being joyful all the time. Bliss must be defined differently for every individual. Some men and women find great joy in cooking, while others find it repulsive. I define *living my bliss* by doing those things that I hold great passion toward. My *bliss* may be found in *undoing*—saying yes or saying no. Bliss is found in the moments of living out the inner boil that fuels my desire. I'm not talking about sporadic compulsiveness. I'm talking about finding a way to externalize my joy for living: by embracing the fantasy and turning it to reality, and by taking on the adventure that I am drawn to even though it is not clearly defined. Here are some examples:

While enjoying a hot fudge sundae at a Dairy Queen in Wisconsin, I fortuitously reacquainted with Terry Kringle (my seventh-grade algebra teacher). A message that I grew up with was that I was stupid and slow. I remember too well how I agonized over the abstraction of a + b = c and why other kids seemed to jump into homework assignments with eagerness that was beyond any understanding for me! Letters and numbers in my world did not belong together, especially in the same context. Why did others seem to *get* what made absolutely no sense to me?

Math in any form for me was like asking me to empty the ocean with a cup! I was overwhelmed and confused by the task of solving for "n." In my evolution to know myself better, I seized upon the opportunity to prove to myself that a longtime belief of being stupid wasn't true. I asked Terry Kringle if he would help me prove to myself that I wasn't stupid. At first, he gave me a look of bewilderment that suggested I had three eyes and a horn protruding from my forehead. I issued to him a proposition that if he would tutor me in algebra, I in turn would teach him and his wife to ballroom dance. *Educators seem to never give up on their students at any age because he agreed to help me.*

Tuesday mornings at my apartment became math class. After a few weeks, the language of algebra was becoming easy for me to decipher and my homework assignments were all correct. Terry Kringle mentored me in more than algebra. He modeled patience and acceptance of my odd request, which was a blessing that has altered the course of my life. We shared the mutual benediction of affecting one another. He affected my *false belief* into the *true message* that I was not stupid; I simply *think differently* than others do. He honored my request for help, and I in turn will always honor his allegiance to education and for the fostering of my positive revision. Bliss then became my *unlearning* and re-*framing.*

When I was studying dance as a choreography and performance major in Madison, Wisconsin, I attended a master class taught by Randy Duncan, the director of Joseph Holmes Dance Company out of Chicago, Illinois. The class was energizing and exciting. The material taught was fresh and creative, and *made my body smile* while executing it. I was mesmerized, enchanted, and happily hooked on dance!

Near the end of the workshop, he offered a friendly invitation to take class with his company in Chicago if I was ever in town and he thanked me for my work.

Guess who took him up on that offer? *I didn't know that it was professional courtesy and not an authentic invitation!* Some months later, there I was heading south to Chicago to study with the Joseph Holmes Dance Company.

It was dark out, and I was in the southside of Chicago searching for a man's home whom I did not know but wanted desperately what he had to offer me. Street signs were missing from the poles and I had to ask a cab driver to help me find my way. I felt like a child at Christmas waiting to tear open his presents while I walked up the steps of this huge white house surrounded by wrought-iron steel. I was met by a fellow company member at the door. His look was a mix of startled disbelief and what was this strange man doing on the front porch, dance bag in hand at seven o'clock at night? I told him who I was, why I was there, and asked if Randy was home. Not only was I invited in, but I spent the night, ate breakfast, took class all weekend, and was welcomed like a friend by the entire company. Looking back, I can only imagine the shock and bewilderment the members of Joseph Holmes Dance Company must have had upon seeing me show up for class with them on a Monday morning, especially Randy!

My innocence, naivety, and passion for dance lead me to another stage of my bliss in the location of Chicago, Illinois. I remember that while in class, and during the return home alone, my eyes began welling up with tears of joyful fulfillment. I felt specially blessed and fortunate to have shared the same space with greatness. I was *living my bliss* before I even knew what it meant! *Men and women sometimes never realize the profound impact they have on others' lives by simply being invitational.*

Searching for a language of my heart, I read an extensive amount of work by Dr. Robert Moore. A phone number appeared in the notes of the last page of one of his books. The book was published in the 1980s so I held doubt that the number was in service. I resonated so much with his perspectives of archetypal hardwiring that I added his name and number to my address book on my phone. I called the number and his voicemail prompted me to leave a message, so I did.

Months and months passed, and I never received a call or acknowledgement that I had called. I resigned myself to the thought that I more than likely wouldn't gain an audience with the man who gave my heart its language. I was a bit sad about that prospect, but I had been disappointed before and came through intact, so I let the idea of meeting him diminish.

The phone rang after my wedding, during my honeymoon drive across America. Dr. Moore received my message, and it was *another beginning of self-discovery, reclaiming, and severing.*

Spending what I would define as *sacred* time each month at his home in Chicago was a gift that to this day keeps giving lavishly. It is unnerving yet liberating to be read like a book by someone whom one barely knows. The skill of Dr. Moore's active listening and discernment through my word choice while speaking was nothing less than shocking and astonishing. I remember well saying to him while in session, "How do you know that?" and his answer was, "You just told me"! It is true that your words either *acquit* or *condemn.* Nothing was taboo in our monthly dialogues and over time Dr. Moore helped me to discover many things about myself that I had no clue of knowing. Among the greatest gifts received from him was that he would never give direct answers to my questions. At first, I was frustrated with him concerning this because, in my mind, that is what I was visiting and paying a hefty fee for! But then one day, after I asked him a question, he stated, *"Look, I'll play Merlin for you, and point out the possible road blocks and dangers in your journey, but you have to answer your own questions by searching within yourself."*

"If I tell you what the answer is, that's my answer not yours." I began to see Dr. Moore with a much different lens. He was a great mentor. He held strong boundaries between guru and mentor. He made it clear that I was not to idolize him or put him on too high a pedestal. He was merely there as a conduit for helping me to discover more about myself and *finding my bliss.*

There are five aspects of blessing energy according to Dr. Moore. One aspect is speaking words of affirmation over someone, and another is to *stand with* a person in their quest or circumstance. He was a generous *"doler"* of all five aspects on my behalf, but the two I listed here were *"Treasures that moth and rust will never destroy."* *Bliss* for me in these special times shared with Dr. Moore was his *Father's heart* for guidance, and his *"Wolf's eyes"* for seeing beyond the veils of my illusions and seeing also my inner brilliance that I was not remotely aware of. Dr. Moore gave me permission to claim my authenticity without fear of grandiosity. Among his last words to me before he passed was, *"Stop refusing."* I knew instantly the context of which he meant that for me and it is a constant voice gently reminding me to *"be who I am."* I often wonder how many other men and women long to hear those words after so many years of trying to *fit in,* by *being who they are not.*

There is a movie that illustrates perfectly the living of one's bliss. That movie is *October Sky* and is a biographical look at Homer Hickman's refusal to follow in the footsteps of his coal mining father. Homer was inspired by the Sputnik 1 satellite, and rocketry becomes his passion. It is the story of a *great mind meeting with violent opposition* from status quo arrangement of cultural norm. This movie also represents the daring educator that comes under fire for fueling the dreams of a young man's heart. The movie further illustrates the call to adventure, the initial refusal of the call, the answer to the call, and the allies that appear as helpers once the *Vision Quest* has been clearly accepted. This is an inspiring account of youthful bliss and *Rite of*

Passage, leading to a man's destiny that changes the world forever. In this case, bliss was not wasted on the youth. Educators, parents, and those in hierarchical roles should pay close attention to what and how they foster the attitudes, beliefs, and values of those under them.

Masculinity is under attack once again. Political ideology is driving an agenda of gender confusion and fallacious sophistry. There is an attempt being made to rewrite the defining qualities of gender that is not scientifically based, but rather is predicated on *emotional* leanings and choice of what an individual identifies with personally. I witnessed recently an interview of a grown man dressed as a ten-year-old girl because he wanted to remain a child as a female. X and Y chromosomes seem to no longer matter, and *mature masculinity* is under attack and threat of being wiped out by the ubiquitous forces of ignorance and misunderstanding. Let me be clear that, indeed, we must embrace the LGBT community. There is great need for meaningful dialogue to take place between the heterosexual and alternative cultures. The Native American culture acknowledges transgenders as "two spirits." Transgender people need to be accepted as human beings first, above our understanding of their lifestyle. Simmering in the paradoxes of life can become the promised land for greater understanding of what we find perplexing. I do believe that making these important choices should occur at the age of legal responsibility with much consideration of ramifications and plenitude of counseling.

Attitudes, beliefs, and values create perception. Perception dictates the reality in which we live. Single mothers cannot *adequately* raise a son into *mature mascu-linity.* "Why?" you may ask. Because they are not male, nor do they adequately understand the *hardwiring* of masculine energy. There is nothing innate or intrinsic for a female teaching a *son* how to be a man. Conversely, the same is true for a man teaching a *daughter* in becoming the fullness of a woman. That is why the structure of a family unit is so important. Something *innate* is missing without the balance of male and female energies fostering the mental, physical, and spiritual growth of children. I am completely aware that some who have just read this are writhing and steaming about my statement. The difference we are expos-ing is the question: "Do we want our progeny to thrive, or merely survive?" Is popularizing a lifestyle becoming the *counterfeit* for *authentic* identity? If identity is made by choice, what or who is influencing that choice? There is strong data from various sources like the National Academy of Sciences that suggests that Bisphenol-A known as BPAs are responsible for sparking changes in gene expression, and that early life exposure to BPAs alters sociosexual behav-ior in numerous species, including humans. Bisphenol is a widely used chemical found in plastic, dollars, and receipts. Bisphenol is also an endocrine disrupter that mimics the hormone, estrogen. The FDA considered banning its use in 2012 but was denied.

The data also suggests that BPAs cause obesity, neg-ative brain altering, infertility in males and females, early puberty, breast cancer, and heart disease. Since the human brain doesn't fully develop until around twenty-five years of age, this data raises some relevant questions, don't you think? I researched why the decision not to ban BPAs was made, and the answer was that there was simply not enough data to support the claims raised by some of the scientific world. I raise the questions to raise social consciousness and ask the question like Marvin Gaye in his song pertaining to society and the Vietnam War— *"What's going on?"* reflected in attitudes, beliefs, and values. More than ever before there are *coming out* parties, transgender identifications, and *psychological neutering* of masculinity in our society. There is also a rampant rise in youth suicide rates. Suicide is the second leading cause of death for ages ten to twenty-four. Suicide is also the second leading cause of death for college age youth. If this isn't proof of the *epidemic confusion* and *despair* our youth today are experiencing, then our society is in great denial, or we are refusing to see what is self-evident. Has the internet become the *"mechanical parent"* for shaping the values, beliefs, and attitudes of our youth today? Thirty-two to 50 percent of transgenders commit suicide. Why? You may argue that it is because they need more support for their lifestyle choice. That may be true to an extent, but what if they don't receive that support? Is not receiving adequate support the only factor? What if confusion with *who they are* is the causality of despair so painful that death seems comforting? What is this societal obsession with creating the *Androgyne* outside of male and female covenant?

Masculinity is a set of attributes, behaviors, and roles associated with boys and men. Masculinity is both *socially-defined* and *biologically* created. It is distinct from the definition of the male biological sex.

According to this definition, if there is enough socially injected influence, masculinity can be redefined in any way that social consciousness sees fit! But then there is the question of biological creation. Hormones and surgery can take care of that. The problem is that the external does not dictate nor negotiate well with what's going on internally. Submitting data and case studies from either side of the questions raised will never solve an internal dilemma within the individual. What if popularized lifestyle, *internet parenting*, and lack of masculine and feminine guidance from loving parents were culpable? Would anything change then? I doubt it very much. Accountability isn't a standard that people hold on to for themselves very well. It's a great mechanism for passing the blame onto governments and those whom we disagree with; however, individual choice must accept individual accountability for those choices. That includes the creation of any needed support.

To understand masculinity better, we must look at how *Warrior Energy* shows up in the male and female.

Aggression is the *shadow* expression of *Warrior Energy*. Women and men have both exemplified the *shadows* of *Warrior Energy*. *Warrior Energy* in its positive pole is administered through activity such as tactics, identifying, dualizing, and differentiating. *Warrior Energy* in its positive pole is interested only in protecting and serving the higher or sovereign figure placed over them or those whom they love and hold dear. The *Shadow Warrior* expresses himself through the desire to kill, win medals, and inflict pain, and conquest at any cost. As you can see, there is a great difference between the *aggression shadow* and the *Warrior* archetype.

When the statement is made that *society would be better off without men*—that is a *Shadow Warrior* speaking. Eliminating completely without regard is the *Shadow Warrior's* realm. The behavior of the statement made is the precursor to the action taken! We cannot vote the *Warrior* Archetype out, but we can regulate it. A man that gets into barfights frequently is greatly in touch with his *Shadow Warrior. Pushing against, resistance, finding personal strength,* and *boundaries* is what *Warrior Energy* is all about. Children are testing and claiming their *Warrior* when they decide to do things by themselves or break the rules through defiance. *Warrior Energy* must be developed for a balanced sense of *mine* and *yours* and proper action for attaining. The chronic bar fighter knows how to fight already. What he needs is the venue to exhibit his *Warrior* that cannot cause harm to anyone including himself. There could be jail time, hospital bills to pay, and a declining social life being a chronic bar fighter. What if he became involved in the martial arts where he was taught the appropriate time to fight and the integration of approach (tactics) during the battle? What if he or she was taught that the *true enemy* is the *desire* to hurt and maim and is not the person standing across from them? What if they were taught that walking away from antagonistic speech shows strength and not weakness? What if the learned tactics of the *Warrior* Archetype served for the same outcome of his former aggression? True masculinity is found in that person who has the strength to restrain emotion through the knowledge, training, and tactical warfare of the *Warrior* in its *positive pole.* Victory could be declared without doing harm.

It is the *aggression* in men that women fear. We as men fear the same *aggression* that women often display as well. Neither Men nor Women are the enemy. It is the *Shadow Warrior* Energy of *"aggression"* that is what needs annihilating. We among the human family simply need to find a place for integrating those *shadows* that sometime take us over. There are many ways for doing that. The fact is, a boy needs his mother to learn the intrinsic role of woman for the nurturing, fostering, and affecting that dad may not give enough of. A boy needs a father for proper learning in how to treat a woman, what is required for supplying the needs of his people, and how to affect his son in finding and living his bliss. Mother and Father standing together produce the archetypal Androgyne in the proper way that the counterfeit androgyne of society can never accomplish. It is the balanced blending of feminine and masculine qualities that create true masculinity. Women are right in calling into account the *aggression* of men toward them. Abuse of women is the *Shadow Warrior* in men. More than likely those men who abuse women had the modeling of their fathers to learn from. The *Shadow Warrior* energy is the enemy not the *man.* If the logic prevailed that ridding the world of men altogether would be best for women, then women would also be ridding the world of their collective sons raised to be Mature Kings and allowing them to model what wholeness of masculinity looks like. Both genders must learn to honor one another so that both are honored properly through future generations.

Humanity is a complex society. We must make room for one another in our living experiences and respect personal boundaries of each. Transgender people who are truly *"Two Spirits"* can become the *Elders* for those of us who are struggling to accept them as part of the *Sacred Hoop*. Transgender people must be willing to model their gold for us. Our unacceptance teaches us something about our *Being* and *Knowing*. Perplexity and paradox just may be the proper meeting place for all of us to strip off our emotional armor, throw down our shields and swords, and strive to *live* and *let live* in the *Naked Now* of not finding from an outside agent, but our *own* correct interpretation. As Jesus says in the Gospel of Thomas, **"When you do find, you will be disturbed. After having been disturbed, you will be astonished. Then you will reign over everything."**

"You should be as clever as snakes and as innocent as doves."

To me that means we must do right on behalf of everyone, but not lose ourselves during our movement. After another veil is removed from our spiritual lens and discernment, we are interrupted by deeper amazement and insight. Our coronation and reign start with reconciliation with the larger picture.

I have established a definition, development, and integration of what *Being* and *Knowing* is. I've given personal experience of incorporating those terms in living my bliss and identified what I judge as the major *shadow* enemies of mature masculinity, which is aggression. What I want to discuss now is the practice and embodiment of living in authentic expression of our *Being* and *Knowing*.

Dan Millman states in his book *Peaceful Warrior*, **"The world is a University and everyday life is the classroom."** As I look back over my life, I am struck by the profundity and wisdom of that statement made by him.

None of us know the length nor the order of our days upon this planet. We plan and aspire to achieve and enjoy, but along the way, *life happens.* I have lived long enough to know that living from my belly's fire is never wasted on living small. When I honor my belly's fire, I find my voice in the crowd and I am heard by those who are *my people*.

St. Paul was a tent maker by profession, but advocating Christ was his calling. Albert Einstein evaluated patent applications for making his rent, but science was his calling. These men's *voice within* became their world-changing *contributions without.* Their light would never have been recognized had they given up on living from their *belly's fire.*

All of us are not called to change the world, but does that mean that we should relinquish our right to finding and *living our bliss?* Is making a paycheck and looking forward to retirement all we can hope to have as a standard of successful living? Is that what keeps you up at night with inspiration and makes your heart leap to get up in the morning? If it does, you have found your bliss. If it doesn't, you owe it to yourself to find it.

Is the search for what makes you truly come alive any crazier than what we witness daily in the classroom of life? What is it that you truly want to do or become? What would you be doing if you knew that you would not fail? What holds you back from doing those things, fear? Remember that fear and courage are extreme opposites of the same continuum. Where there is fear, there is also courage. Move the emotional dial closer to the courage end of the pole and put distance between yourself and fear. It is empowering, and it will open the temple doors to the life waiting for you.

What would life be like if you and you alone got to dictate the terms of all negotiations? What if giving up your job painting for a franchise name turned into a sole proprietorship that *revolutionized the painting industry or resulted at the least in a larger salary?*

Napoleon Hill in his book *Think and Grow Rich* wasn't talking about monetary reward; he was talking about taking our belly's fire and **"chasing it as a man seeks a pond with his hair on fire."**

Practicing and embodying our *Being* and *Knowing* begins and ends with having a vision of ourselves so large that it scares us into being more than we think we are. Fear can work on our behalf for affecting positive change. The outcome is the reward for trusting that process of our life when there is no guarantee offered us. In this solitary journey we unknowingly enlist the help of the *natural* and *supernatural allies* that have always been there rooting us on in our ascension. I am living proof of that, and there are many others like me. Be open to your heart's yearning and ask yourself "*Why not?*"

Like any athlete, the most important ingredient for success is to show up daily for practice. Practice and not perfection provides the exponential component in our *zenith* experiences. The next time intuition prompts you to call that friend you haven't talked to for a while, do it! The next time you find yourself daydreaming about inventing something to affect humanity, act on it! Don't waste your wonder and imagination on what might be. *Make every effort to make it happen!* Like Edison, you may invent a thousand ways how not to make a light bulb, but eventually the practice becomes the *apotheosis*. Efforts that come from internal passion produce the royal energy of joy. This is a great start that will surely lead to others in the practicing and embodiment of our authentic expressions.

The sacred gift of life is expressed in infinite variety. Choices made within that variety become both blessing and curse. What I have attempted to provide you with is a way to expand your *Being* and *Knowing* awareness, and ways for alchemizing negativity into inspiration. Providing a clear definition for *Being* and *Knowing* is a good start in the development of awareness and integration for finding and *living one's bliss* (that thing that makes you come alive and is the bringer of the ineffable). I have identified and differentiated between *immature* expression of masculinity and *mature* masculinity, and I have identified *aggression* as the *culprit* of *shadow* expression in both female and male *Warrior Energy*. *Aggression* must be annihilated for there to be any active listening to occur from either side. Remember that the next time you are drawn into an argument.

You are now equipped more than adequately to become your own viable agent in your practice of spiritual artistry through *Being* and *Knowing*. As a fellow practitioner, it is a humbling experience to catch myself not embodying what I have learned. The *inner critic* has a loud voice at times; my *risk managers* within me sometimes subdue my action to move differently. At its most aggressive state, my inner critic becomes an *accuser* and tries to reduce me and my vision for the life that's waiting for me. You know what? *My practice has taught me that those are only small parts of me that need reassurance that they won't be neglected or forgotten. I honor those voices by assigning them a role in my living for developing reverence in my choices for outward expression. It is for the outer reaches of my inner space that reverence must be observed. I am learning the most when I falter. The faltering then becomes a sturdier ladder I climb upon to personal ascension.*

Thanksgiving is now more than one day set aside for holiday observance. Thanksgiving is the artifact of *Being* and *Knowing.*

Excavating the True Self

Throughout the history of the world, mankind has asked of themselves questions pertaining to their origin and being: *"Why am I here," "Who am I," "Who am I really," "What is my purpose," "Is there really a God?"* The list of queries about identity and origin can be quite extensive.

I remember as a younger man, after returning home from military service, being overwhelmed with reconciling where my place in the world existed after military service. I asked my Dad, *"Dad, have you ever wondered yourself who the hell you really are?"* I remembered him smiling at me almost admiringly and saying, "That's a good question, and yeah, I guess I have."

Most people, to one extent or another, have had moments where these and many other questions of identity and origin have boiled up from a depth within themselves that was unknown to them previously—perhaps triggered by a restlessness and quiet discontent.

I would like to share from my experiences some breakthroughs for excavating my truer self and finding some of the answers to the questions that were causing my restlessness and apprehension for my future existence. I wanted more out of life than a good paying job. What I wanted was a *passion* for living. But how does one find that?

There are some things to consider in finding that passion for excavating your true self. A great place to start is by embracing your idea of the perfect vision of yourself. *What does that look like? How much different does that look from the way things are now in your living? Are you wiser, thinner, healthier?* Simmer in the question of this for a while and get a clear vision of what you want to thoroughly embody as a perfect vision of yourself.

The next thing to do is to believe you can become it by creating a belief system that supports your vision. Use the reverse of "seeing is believing" by believing first that you are that vision so that you will see it manifest. In other words: *Believing is seeing, not the other way around.*

For achieving your goal of your vision, you must become willing to undertake unconventional processes for becoming that belief of vision for yourself. You may do this by any number of ways: analyzing your dreams, bumping up your prayer life, going on a Vision Quest, meditation, and having an active imagination. These are a few of many designs you can begin with. You will find that starting is the most difficult, but once you do, the way you start leads to many other roads of delightful discovery.

As a part of the path to a *greater you* is this: Realizing and embracing the truth that the journey never ends. There are only new beginnings that lead to deeper *self-realization* and *constant becoming*!

To embrace the version of yourself that you wish to become requires the death of the *myth* you were born into, and the formulation of the *myth* that you wish to become. Let me clarify the misunderstood term of *myth*. According to Joseph Campbell, a myth represents an organization of symbolic images and narratives, metaphorical of the possibilities of human experience and the fulfillment of a given culture at a given time. Myth is a metaphor. "John runs like a deer" is not the metaphor. "John *is* a deer" is the metaphor.

"The first function of mythology is to arouse in the mind a sense of awe in one of three ways by moving out, moving in, or effecting a correction" (Joseph Campbell).

Creating a new belief requires a new metaphor that serves as an agent of correction from the old metaphor that keeps you stuck. Moving out of the old message, whatever that is, and moving into the newly created message from the dormant yet authentic heart that previously had no voice is a way of manifesting a new belief and as a living metaphor. In short, there must be a new myth and metaphor embraced that contains all the wonderful qualities desired. This must become your narrative.

Belief comes by *believing* it first and *seeing* it as it unfolds. Desire alone is the one ingredient that guarantees success or failure in many undertakings. If I believe I can't, then I won't. If I believe I can, I will. Think about a time in your life that you were minimized by your peers or parents and you proved them wrong. *What was the force that carried you through to the end? Was it talent or desire?* You more than likely held a firm belief within you that you could and would.

Sometimes it takes unconventional means to break through the noise of apathy, ridicule, and lethargy to arouse the awe needed for the summitting experience. Analyzing your dreams, Vision Questing, creating ritual space for prayer, meditation, and silent reflection are among many processes available to shift your consciousness for believing and seeing that greater version of you. They can be the greatest gifts that you can give to yourself without any remorse of cost or time. I personally have kept dream journals for over fifteen years now, and I can speak to the value they hold for me in discovering parts of me psychologically and metaphorically that I had no clue about! In these next paragraphs I will share a bit of my sacred soul only for the hope and edification of your soul that you might consider taking the "Hero's Journey" by Vision Quest, and learn to listen to your heart, that has reasons that reason itself cannot know, or by analyzing a personal dream and unlocking its subconscious message.

"Dreams are private myths, and myths are public dreams" (Joseph Campbell).

In my dreamtime I saw a great bear; I believe it was a Kodiak or Grizzly. I know that it was not a Black or Brown bear because its color wasn't prominent like its size.

In the twilight heavens, I saw millions of stars and a crescent moon. The moon was a bright silver and cream color and I saw the huge bear clinging to the moon and it seemed like the bear was trying desperately to pull it down to itself upon the earth mother. The moon shifted between a bright full moon and the crescent moon that pointed left. It was a great struggle between the bear and moon. I do not recall that the bear was able to pull the moon down to itself, but I remember the energy and urgency of the bear in trying.

Analysis of this dream yielded much more to me than a greater understanding for symbols and metaphors. I believe that this dream for me was *archetypal* in nature and it is for that reason I selected it. Here now is the message it had for me personally as a subjective dream.

Let me preface my interpretation by first stating that part of my personal work and pastoral living began with dreamwork. I undertook the study of dreamwork both clinically and through the mentorship of Dr. Robert Moore, Jungian and Adlerian psychoanalyst, who has written many books related to archetypal energy, ritual space, and dreamwork, as well as course work from the Christian Leadership University to supplement as a guide and perspective. I would invite you to enlist the help of someone with credentials in dreamwork or a Jungian analyst for interpreting the various symbols, associations, moods, and integrations for your dreams. There are many threads to consider that also deal with the *Anima* and *Animas*. These are the energies of male and female and deal with our personal relationship to each. They frequently come up in dreams and are misunderstood or overlooked. Every symbol is a clue and must be looked at closely.

In my analysis of this dream, the symbol of the bear was a characterization of myself. Understanding the nature and character of a bear, I realize that bears are opportunists. They forage and dig, fish, and hunt, but they much prefer to stumble on ways for their sustenance. They wield the power of instant death with one swipe of their forearm if threatened, yet the multiple stings of honey bees can thwart them from their resolve to satisfy their sweet tooth. Bears know that sugar puts on weight and gives them energy for the months of hibernation. The bear has a reputation for being moody. All this information provides clues that must be carefully considered during the interpretation process.

The moon symbol in crescent and fullness form was the metaphor of change and feminine energy. It is a beacon within the darkness and is the cooling variation of the sun's radiant heat. The moon waxes and wanes during its movement and controls the tides upon the earth. Moon represents distance and mystical powers along with a notion of romance and yearning. The moon is also known metaphysically to be ally to the wolf which, by coincidence, became my chosen name at an initiation of men: *"Medicine Wolf."* The moon also represents something bigger and more radiant than myself. This moon symbol was bright and had no ashen hues like the moon seen normally, so this is another important clue that helps during the interpretation.

The firmament was sprinkled with countless stars and Ursa Major was prominent. The color was a midnight blue and seemed like an endless cosmic blanket that I wanted to wrap myself up in. The heavens were inviting, peaceful, and seemed like home, yet I watched this from I do not know where. The firmament represented to me the vast mystery of the collective unconsciousness, the vault of the Akashic records, star people, and original home. The feeling for me viewing this was eternal, wonderment, and awe.

The earth below represented God's footstool, a place to visit and the home of all creation that does not exist elsewhere. Earth is the below direction from the above direction of the Father Sky and that gives me a clue that the grounding of being on the Earth Mother is to learn and accrue knowledge and that I would still only know in part—the mysteries of life and death. The earth is my humble playground and university of learning. It sustains my flesh and carnal being and allows me footing to explore and understand first the medicine of the Mother Earth.

Taking into serious consideration this information as symbols, metaphor, and emotion, and associating them with my life path at the time, the meaning was also a great blessing:

I am the "Bear." My vision is limited like the Bear, but my instinct of smell and intuitive knowing are what makes me powerful. I am reaching upward into the firmament for something greater than myself, not only for knowledge but to constellate the *axis mundi*. My purpose is to be the center of balancing the knowledge of the earth medicine with the sacred knowledge that is hidden in the Father Sky. I am to dig, fish, and hunt, adding to this knowledge base, but remain humble on the playground of Mother Earth where I was placed. I am exhorted by spirit for not allowing the "sting" of distraction by others in preventing me in my resolve to feed myself spiritual honey representing the sweetness of living.

I am to live in the knowing that, while I shine bright at times, it is not a permanent condition. I will wax and wane just as the brightness of the moon does, and not to entertain hubris as I reach the full moon stages of my living. My power comes from my digging for truth; that is why the neck of the Bear has the hump of muscle mass. Your character can be moody because of your lack of dreamtime. Watch your relations with others as they will judge that you are meanspirited. The swipe of your paw is your speech used. It can maim and kill through reactive tendencies. Monitor yourself, and, like the moon phases, take time to recede, then proceed (wax and wane). The full moon arrives at its appointed time. Don't get ahead of yourself in arrival. Your time is appointed by something greater than yourself. Remember that your animal nature serves you well only as you work toward constellation like the Ursa Major of the *axis mundi*. While this occurs, the firmament yields her secret knowledge to you through multiplicity. You must live in such a way as to reach and grab to receive these gifts of spirit. Live strong! You are reaching for the God that you have not met.

YOU MUST BE THE EVER BECOMING OF YOUR ETERNAL BEING!

To ritualize this dream, I rode my motorcycle to the Apostle Islands at Lake Superior. For hours at a time over a three-day period, I sat in the thickness of the forest hoping to have an up close and personal encounter with a bear.

Deciding to explore the island further, I walked a trail that lead me to a grove of blackberry bushes. In front of me a large black hump appeared from behind the bushes. I had my encounter and it was a bit closer than I would have liked. I was maybe ten yards from a potential disaster. When the bear raised up on his hind legs, my heart jumped into my throat and the pace of its beat almost choked me!

He looked directly at me, dropped down, and ran into Lake Superior for a swim. I was more alive in that moment than I could ever remember. My eyes filled with tears of gratitude for the benediction of life itself, and the presence of a bear in the wild that I could appreciate in natural living. This gave my dream even more power and meaning, so much so that I have an eight-foot sculpture of a Kodiak bear holding a crescent moon in the center of my *medicine wheel* in my back yard. I had a painting made of the same. This dream opened many doors for me on my life path and lead me through its message, to Dr. Moore and the privilege of his mentorship with understanding the *archetypal hardwiring* of human beings and spiritual exploration. Experiences like this one never has to write down, for they are forever written into the tablet of the heart!

Vision Quest

The purpose in partaking of a Vision Quest is what it implies: receiving a vision of how to live in the fullness and illumination of what life offers, by undergoing suffering and severing ties to the outside world, leaving behind all possessions. The main intention and focus is to experience a *ritual death* and *resurrection* during time spent in the wilderness with no provisions or comforts. This is a time for severing ties to unwanted habits, behaviors, or negative thought processes.

Preparation over a year's time allows the initiate to clarify and set the intention of his *ritual death*, and through *resurrection*, how to live in the power of the new vision. That is, if one is given. There is no guarantee that because one takes this *"Hero's Journey"* that he or she will receive a vision. This is up to the *Great Mystery* and your willingness to empty yourself as a sacrifice to *liminality*.

Vision Quests are a *Rite of Passage* that also allows for the distinguishing of boyhood to manhood. This passage is used to claim personal identity and immersion into the community as a man with an equal voice. The *medicine* received in the vision is embodied throughout the initiate's lifetime.

My Vision

In the Gila Wilderness of New Mexico, I died. I presented a small water offering to the spirit helpers and the Almighty as I crossed the threshold of the *profane world* into the realm of *liminality.* It was April and, unknown to me at the time, it was the week of Easter—how ironic!

I went to the place of power I had selected a day earlier. This was a high bluff overlooking the small ribbon of the Gila River. My intention was to heal my wounds of betrayal and ask The Great Mystery to deliver me from the bondage of alcohol. I was lost and hoping to find myself during this time of sacrifice. I had failed treatment twice, was arrested by authority multiple times, and I was here because I had no other choices facing me, save prison or physical death from abusing my body or by some violent means.

I waited for something to happen . . . nothing. The first day was spent in the hot sun wondering and thinking about my life. In the silence of being with yourself alone in the wilderness you can think clearly. There is little else to do except face yourself and ponder how the hell you got here! The night time is when the demons come out.

Every sound and every *shadow* become the metaphor of the fears inside you. *Shadows* loom larger and sounds of nature unfamiliar threaten the safety you left behind. Hopes of safety and vision for life are kept alive through prayer and resolve to survive the *ordeal.* Reality shifts from *monsters* to *God* in a place far from familiarity. Night sounds become the alarms to stay awake and be vigilant when sleep comes calling. The only light for reference are the constellations of stars and moon; it is then the gratitude for things taken for granted emerge from within you. What a privilege to see the stars when everything else in your life seems so dark. Connection to the darkness of self, and the heavenly expanse, give daytime illumination by understanding that they are all part of the same continuum. Sleep eventually overpowered my fear and I awoke grateful for the warmth of the rescuing Sun and new beginning.

Intuition began to take over my rational thought and I, for reasons unknown, began to dig a pit. This was exhausting work as I had no tools other than my hands and whatever nature could provide me as an implement. I looked above, and two Ravens were circling above my site as if they were my spiritual foremen. I became hungry, angry, lonely, and tired by the end of my grave making. My breathing became short, and fatigue from not eating was beginning to manifest.

Nightfall came, and I relied on the stars and constellation for my comfort and nighttime entertainment. That itself was a revelation . . . the habit and need to be entertained, the habit of distracting time with activities. My vision was formulating itself. Questions began to rise within my spirit, *"Where else in your life do you need to be entertained or distracted when you are lonely?"*

"What is this incessant need to be entertained, is God not enough for you?" *"How do these things limit your presence to seeing the world as it is?"* *"Is it not in the silence that you can hear your voice more clearly?"* Most of this second evening was a constant dialogue with my inner man and sacred heart. I began to weep, not out of self-pity, but for time wasted—my anger, my shadowy existence, my selfishness toward others who loved me, but whose love I could not accept. My heart became convicted of the twisted way I loved myself and others. I was a *Taker*, a *Shadow Manipulator*, a *Tyrant*, and *Shadow Warrior* whose pain I wanted everyone else to feel. I thought I was angry at the world, but I was truly angry at myself. My weeping became so intense I could hear my echo in the canyon and my head was a heartbeat of painful thumps. I cried myself to sleep that night and awoke the next morning feeling defeated, exhausted, and ready to surrender to the abyss, God, or both. I was spent. I was all in, and yet somehow inspired by something. Looking back, I know now that I had been given a wonderful spiritual cleansing through the tears I shed. I had indeed that night slept more sound than I could remember. Too many days living on the *shadow* edge of life, I had a hard time sleeping because of guilt, shame, and trying to remember what I had done that I might get into trouble for.

The Ravens were once again circling my position, and I welcomed them as they were becoming an ally of sorts by their regular appearances. I looked from the bluff at the river and it was a beautiful blue ribbon with silver threads from the changing currents. I was being fed by the Earth Mother through the sights of majestic pines, rock formations, and the river herself. I no longer wanted to eat anything. Excess had been my lifestyle, yet here I am flourishing without food. What a contrast of opposites this was becoming.

I walked back to my place of power and the spiritual leading told me to gather stones. I did not understand why, but I was there to be obedient to the spirit's leading and obeyed. By mid-afternoon I had a substantial stone pile. Exhausted and short of breath, my work was about to begin. The voice of God within me spoke to me that I was to take a stone one at a time and place the energy of the individual qualities I wanted to get rid of into that stone and stand at the precipice of the bluff, as I renounce that individual quality, throw it off the edge and watch it burst or crash and give thanks while I watch and believe that the negative quality has been destroyed within me. I began with *fury*, next was *betrayal*, then for *not being allowed a voice* while growing up. Never being *good enough*. This went on until I could not think of anymore. I can tell you that there were no stones left on that stone pile!

Dusk was approaching, and it was now time to enter the *Death Lodge* I had prepared earlier. I had a large stone at the head of my grave that represented the tomb. I realized that as I lay down into this crevice it was like entering the *womb* of the *Earth Mother*—metaphorical, yet creepy. All night until I fell asleep I meditated on the life I wanted. I envisioned a life with no fear of man. I envisioned a life of reclaimed innocence, liberty, and being the master of my soul. I believed in my heart that peace with myself and others is my path, and I wanted to feel alive and passionate about my living experience. I remember saying out loud that *"I'd like to know what it's like to dance upon the wind and embody a peaceful presence like a child."* I wanted to be in awe of the natural world and live natural and free—unbridled, wild, and tame at the same time—wild to explore the unknown, tame to live in good relationship with all things.

I felt full. I had tasted the banquet of nature and my work on the bluff and breakfast this morning was the *orange joy* of the Sun and canyon *shadows*. I washed it down with the refreshing taste of the Gila below me. Awe was visiting, and I was grateful.

After my banquet of nature was consumed, I was compelled to hike down to the Gila River below. I wasn't too happy about this because I was getting very weak from not eating and this was the fourth day. I dreaded more about the climb back to my place of power than I did the descent. I arrived at the river; my spirit welled up with the *unction* to enter it. As I approached the river, the voice within said, *"Take off your clothes, you are getting a baptism of rebirth this morning."* Obedience lead me to enter naked and feeling *a little silly.* Water is a symbol of fertility and spirit, and if God has something good for me in the water, I want it; I've come this far! I fell backwards into the water completely submerged and went limp. I felt *God's pleasure* as I came up and once again I began weeping. Almost instantly I felt a release of energy and a lightness and clarity I had never experienced previously. It was a *numinous* experience of healing, blessing, and renewal. I was in love with myself and my world around me. I had arrived *home*, and *home* for me has been redefined not as a place or geographical locality, but as a transcendent feeling of an *opening heart*. My joy sustained me during the rigorous climb back to my place of power.

Morning broke and I was at peace. I felt reignited by a new energy. Above me once again the Ravens circled, and I couldn't help feeling that something amazing is going on.

Emotionally spent and physically exhausted, I knew my work was not yet over. I wanted to begin sleep early because tomorrow was the day I was to reenter the *profane world* and share with my mentor the *medicine* I received. It turns out Great Mystery had other plans . . . he said, "Name yourself." I began talking out loud to God saying, "What do you mean? I have a name."

"That was the old creation. He's dead. What are the qualities you want to be known by in the resurrection?"

"Well, Lord, like I said, I want to walk peacefully and dance on the wind!" I want to live natural and free and view the world with the eyes of my heart, rather than being at war with it."

"Remember the stronghold table you visited in South Dakota where you placed your foot into the trench the Lakota dug to stand against Custer? Use Dakota in memoriam for those you held dear, and your dogged pursuit to find the owner of the land. That was done in the innocence of your heart and faith. Dakota means peace. Dancing on the wind means you wish to be a Wind Dancer not a Shape Shifter or Eagle Dancer. That is a good name and it came from your authentic heart. Claim your name as Dakota Windancer and begin the journey to walk in the power of that new creation. Never doubt that this is not from yourself but from my anointing from now until forever; you are that man."

I wept again. I felt *sanely insane.* It was now night time and as a last ceremony I made a circle of stones around me and planned on staying awake the rest of the night. Late in the night as I sat within my circle, my eyes became fixed on a small light orb descending into the canyon from the direction of the highway. This orb was bouncing, and at first, I thought someone must be taking the trail to the river and that would account for the bouncing orb, thinking it was a lantern of sort. It was not! Slowly the orb came in my direction and as it got closer I began to become afraid. I lay down as flat as I could to not give my position away to whatever this thing was. As it got closer to me I almost shouted, "Who are you?" but I somehow checked my fear. In about that instant the orb rose straight up toward the sky and flew toward me and passed by me over the bluff I was sitting near. I have no insight for this, but I know now why New Mexico is called the land of enchantment!

Morning of the fifth day and it is time to return to the *ordinary reality* of people and campsite. After a ceremony of song and sharing with a breakfast of walnuts and fruit, my facilitator took me to some ancient ruins and hot springs to ground me and slowly allow me to get back into my physical body for the journey and flight back to Wisconsin.

There is a drawback concerning *liminal space* . . . eventually you must abandon it and return to the *profane world.* Getting back into one's body simply means restoring normal lifestyle like conversation with others, normal activities, and a structure of some type. Oh! And for most, regular eating resumes as well.

I have described and shared with you some of my own personal and unconventional ways for excavating my truer Self. I would now like to give you some insight as to the *"constant becoming"* stage for realization, that the Quest never ends but becomes a journey of how to embody the Vision given and integration of the *"medicine"* gifted during your own *Rite of Passage*, should you decide to answer the call for your own self-realization and excavation.

Liminality is the time of ambiguity or disorientation that occurs in the middle stage of rituals, when participants no longer hold their pre-ritual status but have not yet begun the transition to the status they will hold when the ritual is complete. Another way of understanding *liminal space* is that it is the *"cooking" process* much like the boiling of rice before it becomes an edible carbohydrate. This definition of liminality suggests that even though the participant has returned home, it will take some time for integrating the vision given to him/her. It is wise to be patient with yourself in applying the *"magic"* attained during a *Rite of Passage* or dreamwork. Others may not and, in some cases, will not share your newly found enthusiasm for self-empowerment. There are many reasons for this which I will not get into. What is important for any initiate/participant to remember are the events of their experience and that one should cleave to the messages brought. These are sacred gifts for you and you alone. Someone who has not crossed over the abyss will not have the same skill of filtering the ineffable language of symbols and metaphor that you acquire while fasting or use in Dreamwork. The rational mind cannot understand the same way as *intuitive heart* and *spiritual leading* while encountering *liminality.*

Patience and self-acceptance along the way of *constant becoming* are good concepts to keep in mind. Although in rare cases behaviors have been transmuted instantly, the fact is that most are not. You must remember that training physically takes a measure of time before results can be seen. This is no different in the metaphysical or spiritual realm. You must accept and be patient *"growing up"* into the *new creation.* That indeed is the *constant becoming,* never giving into the distractions of friends or the world that prevent you from being your truest self. I would like to share some mantras with you that came to me during *liminal occurrence.* I hope they inspire you to explore yourself authentically.

"Trying is the indifference of actual doing."
"Trying is the road of mediocre effort."
"Trying is taking the off ramp on the road to excellence."
"Ambivalence is one aspect of psycho-pathology."
"Complacent living reduces great men/women to mediocrity."

Something within you may be simmering that has shifted the thought process to one of action. I hope that it has. I have given a sacred part of myself upon these pages to encourage you and supply evidence of the excavation process and how it works.

Coming to terms with needed change or severing unwanted habits—embracing an authentic vision for yourself and changing the old message or myth projected onto oneself was the first step from the *profanity* of living through the portal of the now *sacred*. I shared through example my own process of creating a new belief system for myself so that I could believe first and see my belief manifest along the way by cleaving strongly to that belief.

Experiencing *unconventionality* through a Vision Quest in New Mexico I gave as another source for polishing the *diamond within* and further anchoring of belief first, seeing after.

I remind you as I remind myself too, that this is a never-ending journey to a *constant becoming*. It is wise to keep in mind that one arrival simply leads us to the next one. There is no time frame given in the realm of spiritual growth. Growth happens despite ourselves; we only need the discernment and special eyes for seeing the evidence of it.

Before ending this chapter, I thought it very relevant for you in your personal growth to see for yourself the actuation of Abraham Maslow's theory during this *excavation* . . .

It may interest you to know that undertaking a Vision Quest fulfills every level of Abraham Maslow's theory that addresses the hierarchy of needs. Therefore, a Vision Quest becomes a personal study of the following:

1. Physiological existence: food, water, shelter
2. Safety
3. Connection/love

4. Esteem/accomplishment
5. Self-actualization

As humans, we tend to be left brain or right brain wired. There are those who fall in the middle and have no clear distinction. For my scientific minded or more cerebral friends I added this as a challenge to you scientifically.

I believe in the spiritual artistry of people. Everyone has a unique perspective and lens for seeing. I am personally taught through people what I want to be more like, or what I want to be nothing like. Either way, I learn more about the man I want to be more like, so it is a win/win.

By now, you have seen the evidence of value in excavating for the true Self. Did you notice I spelled self with a capital "S"? The reason for that is most of us live and die as a small "s"—the self that we were told we are.

I have known for a long time that there was a man who walks beside me that too often I am not. I'm happy to say he is emerging more often lately and his voice is heard not because it's loud but because it is relevant.

Joseph Campbell states, **"The privilege of a lifetime is knowing who you are."**

"*Who do you say you are?*"

"The great metaphors from all spiritual conditions—grace, liberation, being born again, awakening from illusion—testify that it is possible to transcend the conditioning of my past and do a new thing" (Sam Keen).

"Will you answer the call to your hero's journey?"

Thomas Merton states, "**What can we gain by sailing to the moon if we are not able to cross the abyss that separates us from ourselves?**"

"Which distance is farther for you?"

Goethe in 1814 stated, "**And so long as you haven't experienced this: to die and so to grow, you are only a troubled guest on this dark earth.**"

"Is it time perhaps for some illumination?"

Bill Moyers stated in 1991, "**Modern society has provided adolescents with no rituals by which they become members of the tribe, of community. All children need to be twice born, to learn to function rationally in the present world, leaving childhood behind.**"

"What's at risk for you to die and be resurrected?"

In conclusion, I offer these words:

Find your voice and you will find your passion. Your voice is found through silence of the heart in deep contemplation and introspection, not by talking. This will open entrance into the *Kingdom of Heaven.*

For me, the Kingdom of Heaven is known as the meeting place where all thought, emotion, and consciousness form an alliance in the purpose of creating Magnetic Center. It is the human experience of Divine Love and culmination.

"Die well," my friends and fellow travelers so that you may find your bliss and be resurrected to a numinous living experience!

"If the fires that innately burn inside youths are not intentionally and lovingly added to the hearth of community, they will burn down the structures of culture, just to feel the warmth" (Meade 1993).

Self-Realization as Systemic Study

In the temple of Apollo at Delphi, located in Greece, are the words "*Gnothi Sauton*," when translated means, "Know Thyself." These words come from an ancient source and lie at the root of all philosophy.

Uncovering the mystery of my "*true identity*" has been a question I have lived with since boyhood.

I surmise that I do not stand alone in that existential query. Most people have probably wondered, "*Who they are without their story.*"

Knowing yourself, self-realization, enlightenment, however one wishes to define the outer search within their inner space, is deeply personal and is not a one size fits all endeavor.

The main topics of this chapter are best illuminated by Marianne Williamson in her book, *Return to Love*: ***"Our deepest fear is not that we are inadequate. Our deepest fear is that we are powerful beyond measure. It is our light, not our darkness that most frightens us. We ask ourselves, who am I to be brilliant, gorgeous, talented, fabulous? Who are you not to be? You are a child of God. Your playing small does not serve the world. There is nothing enlightened about shrinking so that other people won't feel insecure around you. We are all meant to shine, as children do. We were born to make manifest the glory of God that is within us. It's not just in some of us; it's in everyone. And as we let our own light shine, we unconsciously give others permission to do the same. As we are liberated from our own fear, our presence automatically liberates others."***

This quote sums up the essence of the life examined, and the life self-realized. As an approach to your own self-realization, I am giving a possible direction for you to get started on, and for tapping into potentials and "inner gold" that has been hidden in the muck and mire of false teachings, beliefs, attitudes, and values, and even your own personality. Here then are some branches to the *tree of new life* and a *well* to pull some *fresh water* of thought from.

Many systems exist that a seeker of truth, understanding, and self-realization can investigate for learning and personal growth. These may include a comparative religion study, psychoanalysis, dreamwork, meditation, prayer, the Enneagram, among many others. The point is to look for opportunity everywhere, and in the places you might think that you would not find something golden!

You may also want to continually remind yourself that the search for developing the best version of yourself is a never-ending journey of *constant becoming.* It is a *marathon* that requires endurance and stamina of spirit, as opposed to a *sprint* for instant reward and accolade.

Attitudes, *beliefs*, and *values* are components that shape our reality. We must be willing to examine these with honesty and entertain some *cognitive dissonance* as we wrestle with reconciling our newly found truths and insights about ourselves.

One other thing that I would extend an invitation to you is to consider entertaining the possibility for integrating some "positive disintegration" or unlearning.

This systemic study is the *cave that most people fear to enter* and unfortunately for them . . . never find their greatest treasure. If you are willing to enter, then we can begin the adventure with a question . . .

Where does one begin on the journey to know thyself or self-realization?

Seekers after truth often start from wherever they are. If you are a Muslim, Christian, Buddhist, or Atheist or neither of these, you can begin by examining what you believe, and why you believe that, within the framework of what is already familiar to you. You can challenge what you believe and why by studying what is unfamiliar. This opens the mind and heart to a deeper perspective of understanding without necessarily judging, and it broadens the color palette of viewpoint. I believe firmly that when the student is ready to learn, the teacher appears. This phenomenon has occurred more than once during my continued search for truth. The point is, it is unique to every individual. Searching for truth doesn't require a guru, but you may choose to have one. A support system of some type would also be wise to obtain for use as a sounding board for insights gained along the way, but the fact is the pilgrimage is a solitary journey, and teachers in one form or another will appear either through consequence, pain, joy, or in the real flesh. Learning will be instantaneous simply by starting.

Religions are a system of the inward journey to realizing the *Self.* Ancient wisdom through meditation of scripture and a deep devotion to walk and commune with God worked for many of the early Patriarchs and Matriarchs who shaped the worlds belief systems. *If it worked for those folk, then why not you?* If you are a religious person, you may want to start there, but don't be surprised if it leads you to other places or evolves so much that you begin to question what you previously believed to be true. **"As seekers of truth and self-realization, we must joyfully go into the caves we fear to enter because that is where our greatest treasure lies"** (Joseph Campbell).

There is much wisdom and personal metaphor to glean from organized religion in any denomination. It is wise to keep in mind that every organization has its own *shadows* and *shadow projections*, just like people do. There is good theology and bad theology. Sometimes mainstream religion prevents a true spiritual experience from occurring because of the concretized way of presenting the spirituality it professes. What often occurs instead is a government of rigid defining of ineffable transcendence. *Denotation* rather than *connotation* ruins the religious experience. Let me be clear that I am not attacking the Church or organized religion. What I am saying is that all too often believers with great enthusiasm rush to be held in the secure embrace of God through the medium of the Church and find the rebuke of man-made religion. Rules, and regulated spirituality, along with fundraising and busyness, replace the transformational experience or liminal *space* of meeting with the *un-nameable* ALL! The journey according to scripture is solitary. One only needs to follow the example of Jesus the Christ to see that. Your Christianity doesn't have to look like anyone else's. *Fellowship* is one thing; *self-realization* is another. You can have both, but they aren't necessarily found in the same place! I am grateful for the scriptures of all religions. Scripture teaches me that I am the embodiment of all my ancient ancestors. Name a figure in the Bible, and I am that! I have come to believe the Bible is not so much about chronology and history as it is about the understanding that I am the sum of those many ordinary people who did extraordinary things during their time on the planet. The story contained within the men and women of the Bible is the *story of us*, and the many qualities and parts that make us *who we are!* And yet that understanding takes me to another realm of search within Erik Erikson's work. In the Gnostic Gospel of Thomas, Jesus said, **"Split a piece of wood and I am there." "Lift up the stone and you will find me there."** This suggests that you will find divine status everywhere you look. You waste no effort in the search. Now back to Erikson . . .

Another paradigm that might lead the way to better *Knowing Thyself* is found under the *stone* of the nine stages of psychosocial development. In this psychoanalytic theory, Erikson presents a series of eight stages in which a healthy, developing individual should pass through from infancy to late adulthood. This study is more comprehensive than I can provide as I am not an expert on his work. What I want to provide is the outline to his brilliant work and provide the reader with some keys for unlocking the further mystery of *why we are who we are, and how we turned out that way.* Understanding this will be a great help to understanding our personality development, attitudinal alliances, and belief systems. I would like also to provide a contrast to this with Dr. Robert Moore's work on the *archetypal system self,* and how that relates to Erikson's work.

Erikson maps the early stages of growth and assigns a virtue, psychosocial crisis, significant relationship, existential question, and example for each stage of growth starting from birth to death. For instance, from zero to eighteen months the infant virtue sought after is hope.

Psychosocial crisis is basic trust vs. mistrust.
Significant relationship is Mother.
The existential question asked is: Can I trust the world?
Example: Feeding, abandonment

Seven more stages like this remain, each stage supplying the same example shown, with of course separate virtues to be attained as well as differing psychosocial challenges, relationships, existential questions to be answered and examples given.

Infancy to early childhood, preschool, school age, adolescence, early adulthood, adulthood, and maturity are given approximate age timelines for the individual to confront each stage of development for that crucial point of their living experience.

To give a clearer picture as to how this paradigm can be of help, I will offer the following example starting at early adulthood, given by Erikson.

The existential question asked by oneself at this stage is: *Can I love?* This is a time for the intimacy vs. isolation conflict to be resolved. Identity vs. role confusion is coming to an end, though it still lingers somewhat. Young adults are still eager to blend their identities with friends. They want to fit in. Erikson believes we are sometimes isolated due to intimacy. An Example of this may be the fear of being turned down or our partners breaking up with us. We are familiar with pain, and to some of us, rejection is so painful that our egos cannot bear it. Erikson also argues that "intimacy" has a counterpart: "distantiation," which means the readiness to isolate and, if necessary, to destroy those forces and people whose essence seems dangerous to our own, and whose territory seems to encroach on the extent of one's intimate relations.

Once people have established their identities, they are ready to make long-term commitments to others. They become capable of forming intimate, reciprocal relationships (e.g., through close friendships or marriage) and willingly make the sacrifices and compromises that such relationships require. If people cannot form these relationships, perhaps because of their own needs, a sense of isolation may result, arousing feelings of darkness and angst.

Perhaps you can surmise by this example given that if the proper conditions are not met during the development of each stage there will be a *split* within that individual, and a *shadow expression* formulated. We as humans must presume that somewhere during our development all the proper conditions were not met. This is not to suggest that our parents or sovereign figures put over us failed, moreover they themselves have been handed down from generation to generation the *shadows* or oversights of their sovereigns over them! In truth, we all fall short of perfection. What is important in this example and Erikson's work in general is that we have a chronological map to trace what phase or phases of our lives have need for further development or a clearer answer to the existential questions we may have not had the answer to previously, or the wisdom to ask ourselves.

The capstone of Erikson's work comes through his wife, Joan, who added a ninth stage in *The Life Cycle Completed: Extended Version*. She was ninety-three years old when she wrote about the ninth stage. Joan Erikson showed that all the eight stages *"are relevant and recurring in the ninth stage."* In the ninth stage, the psychosocial crises of the eight stages are faced again, but with the quotient order reversed. As an example, in the ninth stage, *"elders are forced to mistrust their own capabilities because one's body inevitably weakens."* Yet, she asserts that *"while there is light, there is hope"* for a *"bright light and revelation."* She offers the reverse examples for each of the eight stages during the maturity phase. These examples serve to give the reader an overview as to what you can expect to learn and glean for yourself in a personal study of your own life stages to present.

I invite you to download Erikson's stages of psychosocial development for a more comprehensive look at his and his wife Joan's work. It is simple to understand and brilliant all in one! What a privilege to be able to map from the beginning forward, and from the ending of life backward for greater understanding of ourselves and what might have happened along the way to where we are personally through this paradigm.

Looking at Erikson's work, I noticed that the beginning stages of life contained the *archetypal energies* of the *Warrior* and *Magician*, having to do mostly with identifying, differentiating, isolating, or detaching, reframing, and optionalizing capacities through the developments of the virtues of hope, will, purpose, and competence. Knowing this offers many clues to further understanding the *archetypal system self* of the King, *Warrior*, Magician, and *Lover* energies presented by Dr. Robert Moore that I discuss further in another chapter. The contrast of Moore's work with Erikson's gives a more vivid picture of the developmental process in general and offers some specifics why one individual grows up full of trust, and another with mistrust, or a child develops a sense of guilt while another exhibit's great initiative. The shortcomings of development in early stages affect the *archetypal hardwiring* in later stages. The *"hardwiring"* is already there, but the question remains, *"How much has it been altered or affected positively or nega-*

tively?" If I grow up with mistrust, my Magician Energy has been exposed only to the negative expression, and not the positive expression of trust. My *hardwiring*, therefore, is operating out of a one-sided inflation without the balancing of the other. This can be a source of limitation during other aspects of development.

The later stages of Erikson's work seem to be focused on the *Lover* and Royal *quadrants* of *archetypal development.* Dealing with the virtues of Fidelity, Love, Care, and Wisdom is about fitting into society and seeing a bigger picture for not only self, but development of a world view. Finding a place in the world and having someone to share that with is the *Lover* and Royal energies in action. Growing older and reflecting on life is the Royal wisdom for affecting future generations with the *"boons"* they may offer the world as decline occurs. The container of these dynamics and energies begins at birth and ceases only at death. Comparing, contrasting, and reflecting on what has been learned and making a conscious choice to embody the "gold" of that knowledge becomes the metaphor for *"Polishing the Diamond Within."* This is the whole point of the metaphor coined by Dr. Robert Moore. Polishing the *Diamond Within* begins with the consciousness of understanding what energies produce which results, and how development, or lack of development, inhibits desired results in a person's life or inhibits the ability to change what is not working. If I learned mistrust, I will easily isolate from the answers others may be able to provide simply because mistrust is more *online* than the ability to trust another. This potential pathology is a wound in the *Lover* quadrant, yet it may serve as a teacher for not entering one-self into a situation without closer examination. Mistrust has its purpose; however, it should not become the rule for decision-making.

Another *stone you may wish to lift* for finding the voice of God for systemic direction is found within *The Wisdom of the Enneagram* by Don Richard Riso and Russ Hudson. This book is a complete guide to psychological and spiritual growth for the nine personality types.

The Wisdom of The Enneagram breaks down the inward journey for identifying your distinct personality type, Ancient Roots for Modern Insights, Essence and Personality, and a Guide for cultivating awareness. This continues the personal study of *you* with Introducing the Triadic Self-Social Style and Coping Style along with dynamics and Variations of each. The Nine Personality Types are:

Type One: The Reformer
Type Two: The Helper
Type Three: The Achiever
Type Four: The Individualist
Type Five: The Investigator
Type Six: The Loyal
Type Seven: The Enthusiast
Type Eight: The Challenger
Type Nine: The Peacemaker

Near the end of this comprehensive study are helpful applications for you to undertake and experience at your own pace and ways to *check in* to see if your efforts of Self-Realization are fruitful and a way to stay on track throughout your journey. With arduous study you will gain deep insight about yourself, and a way for recognizing and typing others.

Unconscious childhood messages, basic fears and desires, and core identifications of each type are among the main themes of this wonderful tool for discovering the inner self that seldom gets looked at by most. This tool addresses anything you could think of in terms of the human psychosocial system, and within this system you will find the correlation to the theory of Abraham Maslow's Hierarchy of needs and Erikson's and Moore's work. This tool provides many questions that you may ask yourself to uncover hidden *shadows* and beliefs that have inhibited your personal growth. Utilizing the wisdom and knowledge contained within the pages of this remarkable tool will ensure emergence of a better version of you. There is much more to share concerning these systems of study I have presented. My desire was to give you some great and trusted resources to *split the wood* and *lift the stone* and see for yourself what treasure has been hidden from you. These are among countless systems you can use for your personal pilgrimage. There is no such thing as a waste of time in the search for developing the greater version of you. I chose to share these because I use them in my search, and they serve me very well. Remember that I am offering only a direction for a systemic study, not any written rules.

If you are like me, the previous examples I gave as a place to begin your search may seem a bit *academic* or *heady.* You may be asking this question, *"What else have you got that isn't so scientific?"*

"Maybe something a bit more intuitive?" Yes, I do!

Active imagination is a powerful tool for exploring the subconscious mind and allowing the intuitive side of the brain to come *online* and help you to *know what the heart has reason for knowing, that reason itself can never know!* By the way, in case you don't know which side of the brain that is . . . it's your right side!

Have you ever wondered what the color black feels like and what shape it has? Imagine that now. Is it large and jagged, or small and round? Explore this now. *Does that color have a message of some type, and a script or narrative? What does that feel like? Does it have a taste? Where is that feeling in your body?* Localize it until you find a place in you that it exists. This is Active Imagination. *Journaling* after pondering the associations you make with these findings is a gateway into your subconscious mind and hold a key for unlocking personal insights into your wealth of inner wisdom. You can use Active Imagination in a variety of ways to visit the inner structure that predicts your outer world of daily living. If you are a Christian, you may choose to visualize Christ sitting with you somewhere of your choosing and having a meaningful dialogue with one another. If you are not religious, you may want to ask for a *spiritual guide* or some other deity to appear. What is important for this to take place is to use the capacities of your imagination to make it as vivid, evocative, and lucid as possible. Entering Active Imagination is about utilizing every sense object available for creating a detailed and scintillating vision of that time and place. When you arrive at that meeting place, you will want to ask the questions that you want answers to. If you are not sure what to ask, a good one I use is this: "*What is in my heart today?*" After my dialogue is finished, I *journal* what has been revealed to me. Doing this gives me a record of the wonderful insights that I have tapped into and serves as a source of inspiration when I find myself in times of doubt, feelings of consternation, or feeling luke-warm in my enthusiasm. There is biblical support through scripture for "*seeing with the eyes of heart.*" This will supply you with confidence in knowing that you are living the *active word* of God as you understand God. Like I stated earlier, these are only a few of many ways to systematically search for your own Self-Realization. I believe that the voice of Transcendent knowing is available everywhere, all the time. The key is to live in awareness of that and look for that voice in places you would think not to look!

Any level of accomplished self-improvement is arduous and well earned. I would correlate self-improvement to a marathon race. There is the initial burst of enthusiasm from the starting line; however, it will require stamina, endurance, and great resolve for finishing. I know for me it is important to keep in mind that *progress* and *regress* are elements involved in most processes. I may find myself on the way to triumphant victory when out of nowhere I begin to suffer excruciatingly painful heat cramps! That doesn't mean the race is over; it means that I must adapt and focus on finishing. Setbacks are a gift to some extent; they provide the ingredients that I did not know I needed, or provide the *gut check* I need in terms of my level of desire. My road to Self-Realization is not a sprint race; it is a mental challenge of balancing bursts of speed with times of gentle jogging and adjustment in case I get a *rock in my shoe*. What is great about the race to Self-Realization is that I cannot lose to another runner. My prize is in looking back to see how far I've come from where I've been! I can be amazed at myself for the accomplishment of continuing despite the *heat cramps* and *rocks in the shoe* of life that occurred along the way. I am a champion at living because I am on a road of *constantly becoming*. I am learning to be gentle with myself, trusting the process that involves *progress* and *regress*, and honoring my efforts. I have come in touch with the great truth that participation in life at this magnitude has set me far apart from complacency, apathy, and indifference. How can I not claim victory for myself knowing that?

The true competition of my living is revealed through the parts of me that say yes, and the parts that say no. I am my best advocate or worst adversary. I am in competition with nobody but myself. I set the rules and limits by my *attitudes, beliefs,* and *values*—which brings me to the next part of my sharing . . .

Attitude is a settled way of thinking about something. An example of this is "I can, or I can't." My *attitude* dictates the frame of mind I have for each.

Belief is the acceptance that a statement is true or that something exists. "I believe that the Sun will shine tomorrow." Or "I believe that it will rain tomorrow." What I believe often dictates the action I undertake toward an event or cause. Do I *take, or not take, an umbrella? That is the question!*

Value is the regard that something is held to deserve—
the importance, worth, or usefulness of something, a principle or standard of behavior, or one's judgement of what is
important in life.

Attitudes, beliefs, and values shape our perception of
reality. As we travel the road to Self-Realization, these three
elements are strongly active, and actively strong, working
on our behalf. We may find that from where we started,
these have shifted within us, and we are now experiencing
a *rebirth* of our own identity, value system, and belief system, and our attitude concerning past values and beliefs
has therefore changed. We may come to value times of isolated introspection more than television, as an example.
We may find the benediction in relationship with another,
whereas, before, we valued our independence. We may
have believed that *singular* was the best way to be happy,
and upon entering a relationship, we found the liberty of
feeling loved, and that *plurality* brings great joy through
intimate sharing!

The point of bringing these elements to the forefront
is for you to be aware of knowing that through these qualities, that is how change occurs, how the heart begins to
open where before it was closed. Through these elements
we see the world the way we are and not the way it is.

I believe there are times in life that to claim ownership
and authenticity for my living, I must *unlearn* some of those
attitudes, beliefs, and values that have not served in any
positive capacity. This is called, *"Positive Disintegration."*
This theory was developed by a Polish psychologist and
psychiatrist, Kazimierz Dabrowski.

Dabrowski's theory is a very comprehensive one that contains the explanation of the theory itself along with five levels of development within it. He also describes and defines the term *"over excitability"* and how it affects personal development. He offers evidence for his theory of *Positive Disintegration,* application of his theory to counseling, and more. It is interesting to note that Dabrowski and Abraham Maslow were friends and held mutual admiration for one another even though they differed on certain points. You will see the correlation between each man's brilliance regarding their work, and how they support one another from quite different angles.

The questions answered by Dabrowski's work are why some people seem to flourish during times of conflict and tension, and why others fold during personal challenges. Looking at his theory closely I'm sure will provide you with great insight for your own development. The axiom "Whatever doesn't kill you will make you stronger" must have emerged from Dabrowski's theory. That is my own theory, but I think it is relevant and valid. You must decide for yourself.

The *"Gestalt"* I take from Dabrowski's work is the liberty for dismantling and disintegrating those messages, beliefs, values, and attitudes that no longer serve me during my personal evolution. It is refreshing to have scientific evidence supporting *reasons of the heart* that have been looking for reconciliation and that validates the *inner voice* from the scientific world of theory and research. *Is it possible that intuitive knowing can stand side by side with science?* I say it can, because for me it has!

I would like to offer one of many examples I can provide for integrating *Positive Disintegration* in my own living. Doing this has provided me with the alchemy I needed for re-framing a false belief and has shaped a better understanding of myself.

When I was a young boy, I remember how learning to tie my shoes was a daunting task. Mathematics and science didn't make sense to me, and I struggled during all my years of formal education with those two subjects. *I did, however, master tying my shoes.* Nowadays Velcro replaces that challenge; I could have used that invention back then!

The message I grew up with was that I was stupid and slow in learning. As I further evolved, this message followed me into the classroom and over time I began to believe that, indeed, I was slow and stupid. Shame became a daily diet within my *mental menu.* I thought that there must also be something wrong with me because other kids seem to grasp easily what I could not begin to remotely understand. Two times two confused me in fourth grade, and Algebra was like asking me to drain the ocean using a cup. I was held back from recess, and extracurricular activities, which amplified the message and *punctuated* my *shame* further.

In the previous chapter of *Being* and *Knowing*, I shared the process of Positive Disintegration through relearning Algebra and from the mentoring of my former seventh-grade teacher. Can you see now that there is an appropriate time for unlearning something, so that there is room for the creation process of learning a higher truth, or something greater?

I have presented various systems of which you can search for personal self-realization, along with the encouragement to enjoy the journey as a constant revelation over your lifetime. I'm confident the lens you see through is showing you how your personal attitudes, beliefs, and values are shaping your reality. *"Positive Disintegration"* integrated even at its most benign form is not only appropriate, but is the conduit for mental, spiritual, and physical alchemy.

There are so many opportunities for you and me to discover ourselves in each naked moment. Emotions are the gateways that open the heart and mind for great revelations about ourselves. Joseph Campbell says it best, I think. **"The privilege of a lifetime is being who we are."** There is no apology needed for your own authentic expression.

There is now no ambiguity for any systemic study of self, in realizing the greater SELF. We know that there are countless systems that we can learn and grow from. *The fun is finding the fit!* It is wise to remember that the race has no ending but only new beginnings. We have seen that our attitudes, beliefs, and values shape our reality, and upon further examination of them we challenge to test and see if they are to remain, or if indeed there is need for a reframe or option that is a truer fit. *Positive Disintegration* teaches us that tension, conflict, and strife can be the promised land for the development of a new lens for seeing and dismantling a belief that was untrue. Alchemy for the body, mind, and spirit is always available through systemic study.

In his book, *Way of the Peaceful Warrior*, Dan Millman is asked by his mentor: *"What time is it?"*

"Where are you?"

"Who are you?"

His answers are simple yet profound: "The time is now, I am here, and I am this moment!"

A place in time is what it boils down to. Now in this moment to be here. There is no way of knowing for how long, so why waste our eternity playing small and shrinking for others so that they feel more comfortable? We are all meant to shine. If we don't rub ourselves through the process of Self-Realization, then *"How,"* as Rumi asks, *"will our mirror be polished?"*

As you can probably tell, I am a great admirer of Joseph Campbell's work. There is much to discover about myself through his lens that has been a great asset for shaping mine. I like how he leads the way of constant becoming with this statement, and I feel it is worth the extra reading:

"One of our problems today is that we are not well acquainted with the literature of the spirit. We're interested in the news of the day and the problems of the hour."

The literature of the spirit surrounds us in the cackle of the Sandhill Crane, the eyes of an innocent child, and *infinite metaphor. Will you and I allow ourselves more time to lift its cover and read between the lines its revelation concerning our being?*

Systemic study is allowing awareness to lead us toward our bliss, in preference to hitting the snooze alarm and only dreaming about it. *It becomes a choice of being the mist that shrouds the moon or shining like the moon itself!*

Sacred and Profane Space

Those people who choose to heal understand so well the *agony of bliss and the bliss of agonized suffering.* Their power is realized through the alchemy of integrating both opposites. Efficacy becomes the worldview of the healed and healer.

Wounds of the past become the *medicine bag* for future healers. They know what it's like to live the paradox of being happy, sad, and lonely all at the same time.

In sacred space, *re-creation occurs.* Everything known is redefined by new experience and perception. Reality can become *unordinary* reality. Singular existence becomes plurality, which is a time of existence when nothing makes sense in the mind yet is thoroughly understood by the heart. The gift of *"coming home"* to yourself is both the *bliss* and *agony* of *learning* and *unlearning.*

In sacred space, your internal circuitry is rewired. The fear of your internal transformer not being a large-enough container to disseminate the potency of *God energy* is a real danger. Madness and genius are twin experiences and the "being" of *betwixt* and *between* any position previously assigned.

My experience of the sacred and profane is the driving force of desire in writing this chapter. Honestly, though, it is the gift of these experiences that compel me to write at all. My purpose in sharing some of my experiences and what I have learned during these times of *liminality* is to encourage, entreat, and embolden those of you who may be at a crossroad in your living, asking questions but somehow the answers are eluding you. Transcendence may be calling you to a *sacred journey* to *sacred space.* Please hear this and perhaps read this again, *"In sacred space anything can happen." It is a ritual container designed solely for losing oneself, thus finding oneself."* Don't be afraid to enter it! As Joseph Campbell says, ***"The very cave you are afraid to enter turns out to be the source of what you are looking for. The damned thing in the cave that was so dreaded has become the center."***

One condition exists for the entrance into that cave. You must go alone; that is the singular. You will never be alone; that is the plurality.

Allow me to share why my confidence is so high for your success when you decide to embark on this journey of great privilege.

I spoke these words to a couple for their wedding. I was honored to be their Ritual Elder and wanted to impart the power of intention by these words: *"For when a heart insists on its destiny, resisting the general blandishment, the agony is great and so too the danger. Forces, however, will have been set in motion beyond the reckoning of the senses. Sequences of events from the corners of the world will draw gradually together, and miracles of coincidence will bring the inevitable to pass." Joseph Campbell. These words were true for me, and they will be true for you."*

This chapter will reveal to you the difference between sacred and profane space, methods for creating your personal sacred space, defining terms of sacred space, and the proper approach for entry into sacred space for a desired outcome.

Time has two meanings or realms when we are accessing sacred and profane space. Most of what we do is marked by time. Time, after all, is money; seconds turn to hours, days, weeks, seasons, and years. *Chronos Time* is the measurement or chronology of days governed by the carefully calculated earth's sweep around the sun. *Kairos Time* speaks more specific to *God-ordained times*, times not marked by the past, present, or future. *Kairos moments*, then and now, allow us to get a glimpse of the other side. We peek around the corner at eternity. We get a glimpse of how God works. God is not constrained to space or time; that is why God shows up when least expected. When we ask for something right away, it might not come. If we don't ask at all, God may show up. It is possible, but not very likely, that we will meet God in the profane space of Chronos time. It would be like calling your full-grown son or daughter for lunch at *your* appointed and *convenient* time. Good luck trying to manipulate the Creator of all that is!

Kairos moments of time are set apart by God to work on God's behalf and ours according to God's will. *Kairos timing* is yours and my birth and the birth of Christ. Help appearing out of nowhere, in a time of great struggle, is *Kairos timing.*

Sacred space is time and physical space set apart for connecting to God, dedicated to a spiritual or religious purpose deserving veneration.

Profane space is time and physical space devoted to that which is not sacred or religious. It's like everyday living without veneration and is mostly secular.

Community is known as the area of everyday living. *"Communitas"* relates more to the *social relationship* between people.

"Liminal space" implies that the high points of living could not exist without the low points. A person cannot know one without knowing the other. It is the experience of *betwixt* and *between* such as a *cognitive dissonance. Liminality* is between the positions assigned and arrayed by law, custom, convention, and ceremony. Liminality is likened to being in the wilderness, the womb, invisibility, darkness, and to an eclipse of the sun or moon.

"Liminoid space" is artificially produced space and time set apart for change of consciousness, like taking a vacation or going for a drive to get out of the house.

It is important to keep in mind that we can create sacred space. That doesn't necessarily mean the profane doesn't occur. While in the daily existence of profane space, the divine can make its entrance.

Vigilance, therefore, is the rule of the day—looking for God where you least expect you would find God.

Entering in, or the creation of sacred space, requires a definiteness of purpose. *Intention* is the word I like to use for this undertaking. It is the work of a good *Warrior* to be thorough in making a battle plan that will assure victory. *Intention* implies definiteness of purpose as *"What do I want to have happen?"*

"What am I willing to do for that?"

"Who should I enlist for mentorship?"

"Where should this event take place?"

"How long am I willing to commit myself?"

Perfect intention stated to oneself increases the odds for a positive outcome, whether it is finding the answer to a question long agonized over or meeting with *non-ordinary reality.*

Intention is the guiding star that maintains your focus of why you are entering sacred space in the first place. *Intention* is paramount and should not be overlooked in any aspect. The more you are willing to dissect every motive and be in touch with the *heart that knows reasons that reason never knows*, then that purity will sustain you should the desired result not occur. Remember, we cannot manipulate God. We can only appeal to God's good pleasure and stand with outstretched arms stating, *"I am here!"*

In case you didn't notice, you have begun to ritualize your living experience when the decision to enter sacred space occurs—something that, I judge, we in the human family don't do so well anymore. *Technological convenience* and *Chronos time* have replaced, for the most part, our liminal experiences. *Ritual* and *Ceremony* will be the subject of yet another chapter, but all I will say for now is that without those components of living, life becomes tedious and profanely extroverted. *Distraction* tries to replace the *"Kingdom Within"* but never satisfies the gnawing hunger to come home in the meditative silence of hearing God's voice cheering us on to the *constant becoming* of *eternal being.*

We have a new language of the heart and mind by defining what is the difference *between sacred and profane space.* Perhaps we can change our perspective of time, in general, with the understanding of *Chronos* and *Kairos* time framings. We are now clear and can set a proper *intention* for the creation of *Liminal* or *Liminoid* space. *Intention,* as the guiding star, keeps us on point in our pursuit of finding whatever it is we really want. By doing all of this with such depth of understanding, we are now ritualizing our living experience and adding deeper meaning to life. Reality and perception are now the hallowed ground for meeting our Creator whom we have met half way with our best intention for intimate dialogue.

It never matters to me where the alcove is. The joy is finding it. Sometimes I wear the *armor* of my flute or hand drum; sometimes I arrive only in the *naked now.* Sitting alone, I beat the drum with the intention of *losing my mind,* getting out of my head to go deep into my heart. The rhythm increases with my heart beat and I use no common order of vowels and consonants to sing my gratitude and supplications.

I am hoping to pray but many times I don't know where to start. The drum and voice get me started until God shows up to pray through me. If I know how long it takes to get there, I know that I haven't left the profane world with its *Chronos timing.* The sacred world opens only after I have *lost myself* to now *Kairos timing* which cannot be measured by a clock but only experienced through God's good grace. It's peculiar too that I know I have arrived into sacred space and *Kairos time* only after I have left. After having arrived back into the profane world of secularity, I take God with me in the nurturing tones of his encouragement. Nuggets of golden inspiration and artistry flood my being like a perspective of Springtime not asked for, but given to me like a *lover*:

> *As salve to a sore,*
> *The medicine of Springtime soothes the soul*
> *Of an angry winter.*
> *Springtime herald's new colors of purple tasting perfume*
> *And raspberry wishes.*
> *Constellations of born again inspiration,*
> *And renewed ambitions . . .*

In my sacred space, God tells me that the *Kingdom of heaven is the meeting place where all thought, emotions, and consciousness form an alliance to create Magnetic Center. It is the human experience of Divine culmination.*

I conclude that I am a very capable *shape shifter.* It is me alone who trades the sacred for profane, for they exist both at the same time. I can have a foot in both equally and walk in perfect balance among the people on this earth. I don't do it perfectly, but I have tools and a good resolve for continued practice in *living my bliss!*

Rites of Passage

On the third day of the initiate's fast, the spirit of revelation fell upon him—saturated to the depth of his blood and bone with the message he had been taught: *"He would never be good enough." "He must hide his light under a bushel or be ridiculed."* Revelation further showed that *he was not made in the image of God but was molded in the images that suited his parents' and educators' viewpoints.* He was not living his authentic passion; he was living as a graven image for validation that always eluded him. Living this mythology lead only to years of slow and agonizing death for the initiate, and *this was as good a day as any to die. Have you ever felt like this?*

This used to be my story, but it is no longer. I am compelled by conscience and experience to make a statement as to why Rites of Passage are desperately needed, especially in today's modern society. *Myths* are the *mental* supports of *Rites*, and *Rites* are the *physical* enactments of myths.

Since augmenting my lifepath with ritual and ceremony, I now own the ability to *look backward* at my life and clearly understand why Rites of Passage have been neglected and tossed aside as a non-necessity. One of the reasons is that they are not clearly understood. There is short supply of competent *Ritual Elders* for mentoring and initiating those who are willing to answer the call to finding out for themselves what their personal gifts are, and for reclaiming what has been taken or stolen through sterile and sanitized education processes, or indoctrination from hierarchy. So much of our personal story has been projected onto us as children. We have been told *who we are* and lived those myths because we had not yet developed any paradigm out of our own experience. We were simply too young to differentiate or challenge those beliefs we grew up with. That is the purpose and magic that Rites of Passage offer us. Whether you were mentored by the most balanced and Sovereign souls, most of what you have become has been shaped by some projection, good, bad, or indifferent. That is not to imply any wrongdoing by anyone. Being told *who and what you are* and all the wonderful and not so wonderful qualities, is not the same as saying for yourself, "This is who I say that I am." Developing your *"truth"* or personal *"myth"* comes only from your personal experience. Rites of Passage provide a tool for testing and celebrating that inner knowing. Crucibles are used to heat elements for transformation of one substance to another. Rites of Passage, in the same way, give us the opportunity to go beyond the story supplied, and discover for ourselves *who we want to become* and the confidence to be that.

During this chapter, I wish to define what exactly a Rite of Passage is, why it is needed, and how it *contributes inner wisdom* and *personal development* for your life path. My goal in this sharing is also for inspiring you to begin to look at ways of how to incorporate it into your own life, a deeper appreciation for its utilization, and for developing a *tool to shape and polish* your personal *"diamond within"* of personal perspective and reality.

A Rite of Passage is defined as a ceremony or event marking an important stage in someone's life, especially birth, marriage, puberty, and death. It is by no means limited to these, however. Important stages in an individual's life can be many and it would be appropriate to mark every one of those as a *Rite of Passage*. Here are some other examples that are not as mainstream as previously listed: *entering military service, baptism, graduation, going into combat, Vision Quests, Sweat Lodge ceremony, Initiations of any type (fraternity or sorority).* The list could be endless depending on the content of one's life. I will broaden and supply my own definition by adding that it is *any event with a beginning and an* end, with *liminality in between, and reincorporation back into the familiarity of ordinary lifestyle.* Liminality is the time of ambiguity or disorientation that occurs in the middle stage of rituals, when participants no longer hold their pre-ritual status but have not yet begun the transition to the status they will hold when the ritual is complete. Another way of understanding *liminality* is that it is the *"cooking" process* much like boiling rice before it becomes an edible carbohydrate.

The *Rite* itself, therefore, is a solemn act, and the *ritual* is the detailed enactment of it. Typically speaking, a *ritual* is a group of actions performed for their symbolic value. Ceremonies are the celebratory sense that features a gathering and honoring such as an inauguration or birthday. Rites may contain members more than one but may also be individual undertakings. Hopefully that sheds significant light on what a *ritual* is, what a *ceremony* is, and what the headline term *Rite of Passage* means. The difference between *ceremony* and *ritual* has been explained hopefully in greater clarity. Many times these terms are used synonymously and lumped together as the same, but by now you can see a clear difference between them. This conjugation of terms has added to the confusion and obfuscation of understanding what a Rite of Passage truly suggests. Many times, words get in the way of what our intuitive sense already understands deeply and is ready to embrace.

Throughout the history of the world, *Rites of Passage* have been an important component that delineated between youth and adult, boy becoming a man, and girl becoming a woman. These *Rites* were specially designed as *initiations* into becoming the *mature masculine* or *feminine* of their respective tribe or nation. It became the threshold of passing from adolescent to adult in terms of individual role on behalf of the tribe. In earlier times it was paramount that youths at various ages, according to culture, were taken from their mothers and *initiated* as men through brutal tests of endurance, stamina, bravery, and skill building. It has been reported that in some female cultures, such as the legendary *Amazon Women,* that to be more proficient in the use of the bow and arrow, some women chose to have their right breast removed so as not to inhibit the drawing back of the bowstring.

During the days of Sparta, which was a part of Greece, boys at the age of seven were separated from their mothers to begin *initiation* into the Spartan army and earning the title of *"Spartan."* This time of testing lasted twelve years, and because of its brutal nature, some *initiates* did not survive the training. Physical abuse, starvation, and exposure to the elements were the status quo for *all initiates.*

In Tanzania, coming of age for boys of the Masai tribe starts anywhere from twelve to twenty-five. They must first give away everything they own. They must then shave their heads, paint their faces with white chalk, and put on black cloaks and ostrich feather headdresses. *Village Elders* then take them to a small tent and circumcise them without anesthetic. The boy is expected to endure this in silence, as expression of pain brings dishonor. In former days, the *initiate* was required to hunt and kill a lion and only then was he declared to be a *Warrior*. Because of the diminishing lion population, this is no longer a requirement.

Within the Native culture of North America, the young boys were taken away from their mothers by *Tribal Elders* and taught the ways of becoming a *Warrior*. Teaching the sacred cycle of life through the medicine wheel enabled the youth to look at life as a journey of seasons and that this journey is a circle, or a sacred hoop. They were taught about the pipe and its origin, and the responsibilities for being a pipe carrier. The Lakota have seven *ceremonial rites* that are sacred to them that include the following: (1) The Sacred Pipe, (2) Sweat Lodge, (3) Vision Quest, (4) Sun Dance, (5) The Making of Relatives, (6) The Keeping of the Soul, and (7) Preparing a Girl for Womanhood.

There are many more *rites*, *rituals*, and *ceremonies* associated with the Lakota people. However, these are easy to research for yourself, and I have listed the *"primary seven"* that are still in practice today. I wish to emphasize that this is a partial glimpse at a very comprehensive and complex subject. My intent is to supply context through the previous descriptions.

"If the fires that innately burn inside youths are not intentionally and lovingly added to the hearth of community, they will burn down the structures of culture, just to feel the warmth." (Meade, 1993)

"And so long as you haven't experienced this: to die and so to grow, you are only a troubled guest on this dark earth." (Goethe, 1814)

"Modern society has provided adolescents with no rituals by which they become members of the tribe, of the community. All children need to be twice born, to learn to function rationally in the present world, leaving childhood behind." (Bill Moyers quoted in Cohen, 1991)

These previous quotes provide prophetic insight as to the importance and urgent resurgence needed in today's *overtly rationalistic society*. All one must do is look at the millennial generation for discovering the truth as to how we have failed them in their psychological, spiritual, and emotional development by neglecting and non-popularizing *Rites of Passage* as a way of welcoming them into adulthood and the community of mankind. *We are experiencing through them the burning of our structures in culture so that they can feel the warmth they desperately crave!*

Ancient wisdom has brought mankind to great accomplishments: the automobile, putting a man on the moon, and most recently, the technological age, but we have found great difficulty in keeping up with the technical advancement. *Is it possible that we have overloaded our archetypal hardwiring in the Magician quadrant because we as a race have become too identified with rationality and little else? Are we not becoming a race that is caught up in deconstructing innate and natural truth,* such as gender? *When feelings dictate logic, isn't it time to examine where the breakdown of balance is occurring?*

Without Rites of Passage there can be no way for the *immature to decline* or the *mature to incline!* Society today is a polarization of maturity in evolution. Rites of Passage provide the transition from one phase of life to another, be it social, psychological, spiritual, or religious. I believe adamantly that the human heart can have no GPS system without the experience of a Rite of Passage. Proof is our crumbling structure of world societies.

Taking a close look at Abraham Maslow's pyramid of *hierarchy of needs* explains clearly the need for individual assimilation of each level. At the base level is *Physiological needs,* the next level up is *Safety,* the next level is *Love Belonging,* and then the level *Esteem:* the capstone resulting in *Self-Actualization.*

Rites of Passage provide every step of this *developmental paradigm* during its ritualization. *How can we expect proper development from our youth today if as a society we are not providing the opportunities of developmental growth through Rites of Passage?* One may argue that they turned out fine without it, but the question remains: *"How much more potential is left untapped or* undiscovered by its *neglect?"* Furthermore, one generation's neglect is exponentially increased in the next. Look at where we are today! Modernity has, arguably, greater *shadows* concerning Maslow's hierarchy of needs than ever before. Technology has made living more convenient, but in many ways it has sterilized the human heart and de-sensitized our compassionate world view. Rites of

Passage provide *reconciliation* and *identity* for individual development of personal worldview.

If there is no *personal polishing the archetypal diamond within*, through use of *Rites of Passage, then how can anyone reasonably assume that generativity in culture will sustain itself?* Men will remain boys, or girls in some cases, now that even the science of gender is being questioned through rationality. Confusion and obfuscation will be the *new religion,* and the *main sacraments* will be *acceptance* and tolerance for *"anything goes."* Without the ordering of spirit that *Rites of Passage* provide, men and women will have settled for living as *glittering generalities* upon this earth, when, with some application of ancient wisdom, they could shine as *radiant diamonds,* rare and illuminating. Powers that are influencing the course and direction of the world are creating narratives to satisfy their own agendas and impudence. Our own Congress cannot agree on much that affects the total population positively. Leadership has been polarized because the values of what is best for the majority have taken a back seat to individual entitlement and personal feelings.

Being offended by others has become an abomination and a larger concern than unemployment, welfare fraud, poverty rate, and homelessness here in America. *We have seemingly lost our way for any conflict resolution, and those programs that are in place are not working very well.* This should be no surprise to us. *How can a juvenile mind integrate mature adult concepts?* Until the youth has been put to death ritually, there can be no room for the mature masculine or feminine energies to emerge. That, in fact, is why these rituals were created in the first place!

St. Paul speaks to this transitional status within the scriptures of the Holy Bible in 1 Corinthians 13:11, *"When I was a child, I talked like a child, I thought like a child, I reasoned like a child. When I became a man, I put the ways of childhood behind me."* Content of character building begins during a *Rite of Passage* and becomes the legacy of not only individual achievement, but collective societies as well. *Ritual containers* made up of men and women who choose to be self-examining will develop the *Kings* and *Queens* needed for our progeny and future. This truth used to be self-evident.

Upon examining and defining what *Rites of Passage* include and what purpose they hold, *can there be any doubt that now, more than ever, they must reemerge in the shaping of our youth to the mature masculine and feminine expression they are designed to be?*

We have discovered that a *Rite of Passage* involves many things, marking an important event experienced like a graduation. More than that, it is a celebration of transition, *putting to death* the *youthful existence* and *entrance into manhood, or womanhood,* and *celebrating that important transition.* This provides the *anchoring* and *full ownership* of *new life* and *identity.* Through the hardship and difficulty experienced during ritualized Rites, the participant has very little doubt they have become a *new creation* through the mentoring of *good Eldership,* the grace of *Transcendence,* and *personal ownership* of their actions. As a cauldron is needed to break down base metals for greater uses, so it is necessary for the human psyche and soul to be broken down from inferior youth to superior adulthood. The beginning of mature adult behavior only occurs with the death of adolescence. This is the purpose of all *Rites of Passage*: transition through *liminality, betwixt,* and *between,* making a conscious choice to remain being *taken care of,* or *becoming caretaker* for the people. Simplicity suggests the question, *If I have not learned to be self-reliant through the fire of trials, then how can I be relied upon?*

Endurance through, and the emergence from a Rite of Passage, has shaped my archetypal diamond within, spiritually, psychologically, and emotionally—equipped to face and withstand the rigors of all life throws at me. Mistakes or failure within that process become the stepping stones for future successes. The connotative adult is now denotative and that is still a constant evolving expression of action and cause.

Joseph Campbell stated that **"the privilege of a lifetime is in being who you are."** Earlier in the book I related a story of who I thought I was from a narrative that was given to me. Something innate within me gave me great cause to challenge that myth that kept me stuck for many years. Campbell further states that, **"Myths are public dreams, and dreams are private myths."** Being who I am, according to the public dream, kept me from the authenticity of my private myth of being who I am. *Do you see how easily that can happen now? Are you able to understand that* Rites of Passage *can change a shadow message into a golden one, and help you to claim for yourself a death to one life and resurrection experience to another?*

I am an ordinary man with no exceptional talents. I know within the depth of my being that I could not and would not have authored any of these words had I not accepted the challenge and freely given gift that *Rites of Passage* offered me. I for one am grateful for any process in my life that enables me to see myself better, and that allows for *transmutation* and *transformation*. After all, as Thomas Merton states, **"What can we gain by sailing to the moon if we are not able to cross the abyss that separates us from ourselves?"**

In conclusion, I would like to invite the reader to entertain this thought:

The *magic* of a *Rite of Passage* isn't held through its form. The *magic* is in your obedience to answer the call for change to occur and following of your heart's leading. The process will be right for you because you chose it for yourself. *How many people do you know who can say they have chosen for themselves the method* of *their own death, and the resurrection of their new life? You can be one of them,* die well . . .

"The great metaphors from all spiritual conditions—grace, liberation, being born again, awakening from illusion—testify that it is possible to transcend the conditioning of my past and do a new thing." (Sam Keen)

Muscarian Madness and the Peyote Religion

"Discernment is the spiritual filter for an open mind."
—Dakota Michael Windancer.

The Hebrew prophet Jonah tried escaping his divine mission by sailing in the opposite direction from what his prophetic ministry was commissioning him toward. According to the story, trouble at sea soon occurred, and it was determined by the ship's crew that Jonah, through his disobedience, was the cause for rough seas that threatened the lives of all on board. Thrown overboard to satisfy God's wrath, Jonah was swallowed up whole by a great fish.

It is the *archetypal nature* of humans to be disobedient at time; this story serves as a warning as to where it may lead—THE ABYSS! Therefore, the only purpose I offer within this chapter is a sincere warning to fellow travelers. Please be careful on your journey!

The *abyss* in this story is represented by Jonah being an unwilling captive within the belly of a whale. I want to share with you one of my *"belly of a whale"* experiences, because I believe it is of utmost importance in the search of discovering our greatest potentials and who we truly are, that we use wisdom along with the *fire in our belly*, known as zeal. My purpose for this chapter is to enlighten you to some *shadowy* pitfalls on the road to self-realization. I believe it would be very irresponsible on my part not to give you a *"heads up"* for recognizing the seductive qualities and dangers of replacing a *"Spiritual Leading"* and nature of being, with *"phenomenology."* My use of this word is meant to be broad, including experiences of sights, sounds, and mystical occurrences.

I do not wish to moralize regarding the use of psyche-delics, Ayahuasca, LSD, alcohol, or cocaine. I have searched for my spirituality during periods of my life experience through them all and found that my *"god"* became the chasing of alternate states of consciousness and phenomenon, every time *leading me further from myself* through artificial distraction and emotional altering. For me, this pursuit of self and God lead me to the *abyss* of addiction—starting out as innocent fun, ending in shame, guilt, jailtime, and many severed relationships, not to mention the strain on the ones remaining. Even in those days I had a *shadowy* excuse, right? Wrong! I was addicted, and that's what addicts do! Even though I made those choices, I couldn't help it, I was hooked. I needed help, but I wasn't ready for it. I was still managing my life so far, and I was still having fun! I was in the *belly of the whale* and didn't even know that I had been swallowed whole! I was in a giant cooking pot and was slowly being boiled alive. Eventually my sleepiness caused by the heat would be eternal and almost was.

It is one thing to get on the wrong path by partying and after work revelry—my temporary demise started out that way. What I want to address is the sober mind that becomes vulnerable to the *abyss* through the means of spiritual zeal, and what happens when the *Lover Energy* inflates without the *Warrior Energy* that provides proper borders and boundaries, or the *Magician without the wise sage* for giving a proper process and approach along with safety. What could happen if we don't access *Royal Energy* for seeing the larger picture and fostering for a blessed outcome?

Sobriety had been great; I was experiencing lucid dreaming, restored relationships, work was my playground once again, and there was now strong hope of the girl I loved finally saying yes to a marriage proposal that previously had been rejected three times. Gee I wonder why? Not really.

Life was beautiful; I wanted to live! I was grateful for my opportunities that I had previously not seen nor had any awareness of. Everything looked different to me, and I knew that I was loved by something bigger than me; the proof was that I was entering sobriety for my tenth year. No booze, no mind altering in any way other than through meditative journaling and lots of prayer—I needed it!

I had completed two musical albums with people I had met through my place of worship. We put on a wonderful concert and *God was in the house!* My life had turned around and I was on fire to know myself more and more, and I wanted to experience that *Transcendence* every way I could.

Amanita muscaria is the scientific name of a type of mushroom that contains at least two agents of psychoactive properties; they are muscimol and ibotenic acid. *Plant people* have *medicine* to give and something to teach. When their secrets are sought after, there is no choice given the seeker as to how they are revealed, if indeed they are.

I enlisted for safety, a man that I knew I could trust and I ingested the mushrooms on the way to a sacred space of Wisconsin that held special meaning for me. Looking back, I believe it was no coincidence that I chose the land where The Battle of Wisconsin Heights, known as the Black Hawk War, was fought in the early 1800s and contained linear Indian Mounds where my ancient predecessors were buried. This was a battle fought for land rights and way of life. I was soon to discover how *symbolic* this site was to become in my search for myself.

The effects were extreme and physically onerous. While at the mounds, I began sweating profusely and lost all control of bodily functions. Before I desecrated the resting place of the ancients I asked my facilitator to help me move deeper into the woods where my lack of control would not dishonor myself, or my relations that were resting. Almost immediately I blacked out and entered what I can only describe as a *shadow womb*. I had no awareness of my physical self, but my altered state of consciousness was terrifying me with a dreamlike narrative that I was *in between* death and life. Spirits of the dead were rebuking me harshly and I believed that I must be in Hell. I remember clearly believing I had died. *But if I died, then why am I aware of my death? Is this the death experience, being aware that you are no longer a physical being separated from the body, yet conscious of nothing but darkness and chiding voices?* I wanted to tell my friend John, "I'm still here, don't leave me." *How did I know I was truly alive if this is what death is like? How would my friend explain what happened?*

While I was in this *shadow womb,* my thoughts went into a review of my living experience and I was overwhelmed with the thought of, so much time wasted and how once again I had betrayed those who loved me by taking a risk that cost me my life and there was no way to explain what I believed was done from a pure motive.

Suddenly I woke up and vomited what seemed like gallons of yellow bile. I hadn't even finished vomiting when the other end exploded feces like a volcano. Forgive the graphic detail; I promise there is greater purpose for sharing in this way. Upon waking up, I became elated and euphoric. I now had evidence that I was not dead. I could see John's face and the environment looked like the world I knew. I lost consciousness again and returned to the *shadow womb.* I believed again that this was Hell's way of *playing with my mind during death.* My soul wailed, and the *weeping and gnashing of teeth* became all too real for me.

This *"Shadow Dance"* continued like this for about six hours. I would wake up and realize that I had not made it any further on the trail out of the woods. I defecated and vomited violently during that time to the point of losing fourteen pounds by the end of the day. I had spent the day rolling around in my own feces and vomit, in and out of consciousness, believing with all my heart that I was dead!

Another aspect of this death experience is that *opposites became the truth.* It was eighty-five degrees that day and I was freezing. Riding in the car, I begged for John to turn the heat all the way up. When stopped at a red light, I was confused as to why he was not proceeding through. *I was in the liminal space of betwixt and between.*

John knew that I must not return home in this condition. We stayed at a motel for the night until I was back in my body and had returned to some extent of normalcy.

When I could finally trust that I was delivered from the *shadow womb*, I was so grateful to be alive that I began to take inventory of my life.

I am either a slow learner, or a fast forgetter, because it only took a year or so to accept an invitation to attend a service held in the *Peyote Religion*. The idea of an all-night prayer meeting with friends and native leaders appealed to me very much since mainstream Church didn't work so well for me. Truthfully, it wasn't the Peyote that seduced me into attending. What I was most intrigued by was what shape and design the *ceremony* would look like. I was interested to know how the *Elders* would be able to keep people engaged and awake all night from 7:00 p.m. to 7:00 a.m. I attended many different ritual and ceremonial events and always paid close attention to the ordering and structure they held. I enjoy creating and being a part of *Ritual space*, especially if it is facilitated well. For me, this was a greatly anticipated opportunity to see how hundreds of years of tradition and practice would unfold itself to me, as a participant.

Peyote is a psychoactive alkaloid that comes from a small cactus that grows in Mexico and parts of Texas. The mescaline within this plant can produce a wide range of effects, both auditory and visual. As participants we ingested peyote prepared as a tea and in a dried form, crunchy and hard. Also, soft forest green pieces of small button-like shapes were offered throughout the entire ceremony.

An altar was made that held the sacred *Channupa* or pipe along with the water drum that was beaten by one of the *Elders* continuously throughout the entire ceremony. Sitting in a circle, we sang songs and offered prayers as the peyote began taking effect on each of us.

Peyote presented itself to me in a very introspective and internally reflective way. I experienced insights about myself that I had not previously entertained nor thought of before. Deep reflection of losing my innocence by making bad choices and the desire for reclaiming that innocence lost was the theme my consciousness seemed to attach itself to throughout the evening. I felt great remorse for losing my virginity at the tender age of fourteen to an older woman. I erupted into a sadness for my irresponsible choice of rushing into a *Rite of Passage* sexual in nature for defining myself as a man. Embracing my carnality had nothing to do with manhood; it was the *illusion* of it. Giving my power over to my sense objects and a woman that I was not in love with was a form of spiritual slavery and prison time in my memory of great regret. I wanted to reclaim my innocence lost but had to settle for a reconciliation of carnal desire with spiritual discipline. This has been a large component of *inward journey* and *external path* for me since.

As the night unfolded further, the peyote started to *get in my way.* It became increasingly difficult to articulate both verbally and mentally. Every time an insight would begin to surface, it would drown in a sea of other *thought noise* rushing in. My body began to become restless and my stomach felt like it had an *iron claw* inside it that was opening and closing itself on the lining of my stomach and intestines. I felt strong urges to vomit, yet I could not. The physical symptoms were starting to *steal my intention* of introspection away from me. I found it very difficult to stay focused on the *within direction* while the *without direction* was trying to raise up and have its say. I realized there was a crazy correlation between the two. The metaphysical principle, "As within, so without," "As above, so below," quickly reminded me that my *inner turmoil* was akin to my *outer symptoms*, and that to *ascend spiritually* I must also embrace the *lower body of discomfort* in physical form. This revelation is a gift that I am relearning constantly.

Time seemed to be elastic. Sometimes things moved at breakneck speed, and at other periods the songs lasted for what seemed like hours. My body was tired of enduring discomfort and I wanted to move. Protocol prevented anyone from leaving unless is was to *"get well."* In the peyote religion you don't get sick, you get well. When a person vomits, they are getting rid of what is not needed; therefore, vomiting is an act of getting well.

Dawn had begun to peek through a small window and the ceremony came to its conclusion. Feasting afterward was as important as the ceremony. Feasting helped to *ground us physically* and experience community in a more gregarious and lighthearted manner. It was like a debriefing after a military mission being completed. Food that morning didn't offer taste for me. Food played an unusual role for me that day. I was hungry, but my belly and taste buds were not in coalition with each other. Food became a necessary filler only. Food offered no comfort for me. That *steel claw* was still opening and closing inside of me, and it

157

was more than a distraction. It was affecting my personality and mood. After safely arriving home, I knew immediately that this was not a ceremony I belong to. This was not a part of my path, not because of feeling I did something wrong; I didn't! I was invited, and it was a legal participation. I embraced this with an open heart and mind. If I could attend the same ceremony without ingesting the peyote, I would, but I doubt that could happen. I am not, nor is anyone else, that special to revise a tradition and ceremony as old as the earth.

Looking for God in all the places you would think you cannot find Him can yield some inner gold for any of us. *But at what cost?* The question that I had for quite some time was, *"Are you finding God in these moments, or a phenomenology of God-like qualities?"*

"Might it be possible to have gained the same or even deeper self-realization had you not been altered by psychoactive agents?"

"Is this a sustainable way of connecting to spiritual insight?"

"What is at risk by continuing exploration in this way?"

"What do you risk if not?"

"Is this community of religious practice composed of your people?"

"Do you know who your people are?"

"Are you called by God to be in Community or solitary search?" These questions for me have been answered with considerable clarity.

I believe that we are all spiritual artists. We are called separately to a collective understanding. *What is spiritual artistry?* My answer to that is a path on which I both succeed and fail.

For me, *spiritual artistry* is the recognition that I am lead too often by compulsion. My belly's fire sometimes leads me to situations through raw zeal without implementing the wisdom of discernment and qualities of my *Royal Energy* for seeing a larger picture and what may be at stake by the choices I make. Institutes and religions all have their *shadows.* Being a part of a community yields both *gold* and *shadow* in relationships. This facilitates personal growth. *Spiritual artistry for me is not taking inventory of religion's shadow but in the inventory of my own.* There is a saying among the *Shadow Worker Community* that, "If you spot it, you got it." *Spotting Shadows* is not a license for judgment of others; it is a way for examining our motives and seeing in ourselves what we may need some compassionate dialogue with. When I can weave my artistry in that way with others along the road, I am co-creating a generative community. Dialogue is easy to have when *shadows are owned authentically.*

The *belly of the whale* is always waiting to be filled by those who are willing to enter the cave they fear the most. When there is a calling to come out and be separate, we must use *discernment* and *wisdom* in preparation for that journey of soul that promises nothing in return, but that also holds our greatest treasure. I would never repeat my undertaking of what I shared in this chapter, not through psychoactive manipulation. That became a *false god* and *idol worship* for me. *I chased the experience, rather than having Divine dialogue.* I am fortunate to have been left mentally intact.

My conclusion is that finding *who I truly am* is a process of time, temperature, and tension. The proper time will reveal itself to me for creating sacred space. I must allow *Transcendence* to cook or boil me to the temperature that will provide the transformation needed. I must be willing to endure the tension of process taking place without always the understanding.

There can be no manipulation of Spirit's expression, only a manipulation of mind for understanding its message. It is my sincere hope that on your path to knowing yourself, you don't get detoured by compulsions and spiritual wisdom promised through seductive whispers that emanate from raw zeal and belly's fire. *Spiritual discernment* is the filter for an open mind. Put wisdom above zeal.

It would be wise before any ritualization to access the Royal Energy for the bigger picture seen, and the fostering, nurturing, and affecting needed during the process. Have dialogue with your Inner *Warrior* and set proper boundaries and limits. In *ritual space,* it can be another seduction to push limits too far. People have perished because they did not regard this! It is important to have a clear dialogue with your Inner Magician and know exactly how you will provide safety needed and define for yourself the logistics. Finally, you must remember to access your *Lover Energy.* Be gentle and kind with yourself. The process you experience may be harsh enough. When you are in the *abyss,* or the *belly of the whale,* you don't get to determine what happens; that is why I hope you take this offer of counsel before you leave on a *Hero's Journey.* You will find that by doing this you have fulfilled Maslow's theory of the *Hierarchy of*

Needs. You can be self-assured and embark on your journey with a better level of confidence and a safe return by implementing the *archetypal qualities* available to you.

Why would ingesting hallucinogens expand my consciousness? Non-ordinary reality does not necessarily denote spiritual wisdom or spirituality in general, especially if it is artificially induced. *Rites of Passage* that do not involve artificial means can result in the experience of meeting with Spirit in a natural way with extraordinary consequence and outcome. *"Rites of Passage"* are an important process and access to deeper personal growth. In another chapter, I will present arguments of why they are desperately needed especially in today's rationalistic society, and how to prepare for your own Hero's Journey in a safe way for better assurance of obtaining what you may be seeking to find out about yourself, and in affecting your worldview. Our spiritual quests must be a solitary effort. We must therefore ensure that it is the Creator we seek, rather than the phenomenology of mind-altering experiences, claiming it as a spiritual pilgrimage.

"Where my treasure is, my heart will be also" (Matthew 6:21). That is why the true God I seek must be first, last, and always. Travel well, my friends . . .

Symbols and Metaphors

McDonald's *golden arches*, the four *conjoined circles* of the Audi automobile, the *gold right angle "L"* of the Lexus. *"Live like a King," "Apple of my eye," "Battle of egos"*—these are common symbols and metaphors that advertisers and marketing specialists inundate us with every day, through mainstream media, billboards, and even through the power of musical expression.

Everyone remembers the call to edible sovereignty through the musical jingle, *"Have it your way at McDonald's,"* or the power-filled voice of Bob Seager singing the praises of Chevrolet with the words, *"Like a rock."* The suggestive nature of these metaphors appeals to our *archetypal energies* of the *Royal Energy*—we can have our sandwich anyway we choose—we are the alpha and we order our culinary universe, and that by owning and driving a Chevy truck, we are operating and structuring our lives out of the toughness and strength of a battle-hardened *warrior*. Our truck is tough, and so are we. *Or are we?*

There is good reason that the advertising and marketing industries spend millions to profit by billions. Symbols and metaphors speak to us *metaphysically* through our *archetypal hardwiring* and emotional states.

If these billion-dollar industries can manipulate us into eating when we are not hungry and buying a truck to feel safe, secure, and better protected, then *how can we as individuals develop our own paradigm of how to utilize symbols and metaphors daily to constellate for ourselves our personal bliss, and efficacy for living? How do I know if a symbol is sacred or secular? Does that matter? Is a metaphor only linguistic origination, or does it occur in nature? Workplace? Or other life occurrences?* What I do know of symbols and metaphor in living is that they contribute significantly in the ritualization of our lives; therefore, I believe it is of utmost importance to become more consciously aware of their clandestine and subtle entrance into our living space, by the *Shadow Magicians* of society and, beyond that, to develop for ourselves a meaningful and transformational integration of our own *sacred* or *personal symbols* and *metaphors* for attaining greater personal power over the unseen forces that sometimes drive us.

In this chapter, we will define the terms "symbol" and "metaphor." You will see that their meaning is much broader than we may have previously supposed. We will discuss and present ideas that support the need for developing our *personal paradigm* of symbols and metaphors and how to utilize them. You will learn also that using the hemisphere of the right-brain (intuitive seeing with the *eyes of your heart* and *dreamtime*) will open the world of symbols and metaphor as well as the left-brain world of numbers and language from where they originate.

One definition of the word symbol: a mark or character used as a conventional representation or object, function, or process—something which stands for something else.

Metaphor is defined as a thing regarded as representative or symbolic of something else, especially something abstract.

Here is an interesting and thought-provoking look at the symbols of a dot and circle gleaned from the book, *Signs & Symbols Sourcebook* by Adele Nozedar: A dot, something so unassuming, yet when looking for it in the world around us we see it as closure of a sentence written, an essential structure in writing, making it the beginning and the end, origination and conclusion containing all possibilities of the Universe within it. It is the spot also where the lines of the cross meet—the center. Dot can be a symbol of the third eye as in the "Bindhu," meaning absolute, placed in the forehead at the position of the third eye believed to be where the seat of the soul lies.

The circle as Sun and Moon takes on a different personification when pondered as "God being a circle whose center is everywhere, and circumference is nowhere" (Hermes Tresmegistus).

Circle can be represented as "something—an unbroken line, and nothing—the space within and without the circle." Circle therefore represents spirit and the cosmos, unifying matter. Since the circle has no divisions, it may also represent equality. Now you may see that *familiar* and *ordinary* walk side by side with the *abstract* and *profound*.

Potentials that exist in the rediscovery of symbolic usage could be infinite. I dare say that indeed it is . . . our work is to sit long enough in *Lover-creative* and *Magician-thought* energies to connect to them.

Perhaps you are beginning to see already the connection between symbols and metaphors. Metaphor becomes the story explaining the language of our heart and landscape of soul that others only see in the boundaries of mundane existence. Metaphor becomes not only a written expression but living experience of interpreting the symbolic world around us.

What are these metaphors and symbols that transpire? What is the significance behind them? How do I gather the insight and *medicine* it is offering me to affect my path of living?

It has become difficult I think for modern society to slow down enough to see the symbols and metaphors of their living emerging. We are in the habit of multitasking, not allowing ourselves to experience the *nakedness* of now. We full steam ahead into the waiting demands of our day through work and schedules, not giving rise to what is unfolding in front of us through the abstract world of symbol and metaphor—funnel vision with little regard to periphery.

Metaphors and Symbols are the realm of magic that spring from contemplative living:

It was summertime in Wisconsin and I was up early to witness the sunrise. I enjoyed watching it slowly break on the horizon with its explosion of reds and oranges within the powder blue firmament. I heard the *orchestra* of at least seven different birds pitching at once, their affirmation of a new day. I remember feeling special in that moment. I was witnessing the dawn and *breath* of new life and felt a special welcoming from it. I was feeling alive and joyful—grateful for my life, the good and bad roads that I have taken.

Suddenly from the periphery of sight, my eyes became fixed on a large lilac bush. I could smell a hint of lilac perfume as I fixed my gaze, and it was then I noticed it was half dead. My earlier inspiration had now turned to a reverence for life. *Intuitive voice within* asked of me these questions, *"How are you Dakota, like this bush you see? How are you half dead and half alive? What parts of you need resurrecting? Are you only allowing a hint of your fragrance to permeate your existence like this bush you see?"*

Innocence of daily living had brought the amazing gifts of metaphor and symbol to the threshold of my heart, and, *dagger-like*, it pierced me deep with the inner truth that I had indeed allowed a part of my vision for living to die. I was not living as a pungent presence, and without question I must resurrect what I had put to death through apathy and habituation of life in the fast lane, a large component of my life that makes my *spirit soar*—writing. That private moment in Wisconsin became indelible and the reason I am writing today. Writing has become one way to remain true to myself; it doesn't matter if my offerings are good enough for anyone else to read. What matters most is that through the discipline and joy of writing I create a world that holds infinite blessing for myself through following my personal *bliss* internally through outward written expression, and for others who may be able to relate to this amazing world of senses, sounds, and smells, and the magic of abstraction found through metaphors and symbols.

Even now as I share this with you, my heart is leaping to the *"yes"* of life. Metaphors can be given through painful experience as well as pleasurable ones. If I seek a life without pain, the metaphor I create for myself is saying *"no"* to the collective of living experience. I would miss so much that way. I would like to think that most of my suffering is over, but I know that it is not. I have learned to ask my Creator to *"teach me gentle."* Pain and suffering have yielded wisdom to me through metaphor and symbol as well. I share this as proof:

I had never been in a canoe, yet I found myself pushing off from an inlet in Prairie du Sac, WI, headed for Spring Green, WI, some twenty-five miles away. My provisions were very light: four one-gallon jugs of water, a small blanket, and a *New International Version Bible.* The remainder of space within the canoe was filled with *trepidation* and one wooden oar. I had but one pair of shorts to wear, no shirt, and nothing to use for shelter.

Looking back, I was foolish and would never repeat this journey so haphazardly again, but here I was undertaking a *Vision Quest* in search of answers I desperately needed. I headed westward, the direction of *magic,* the place of introversion, the *"Thunder beings"* and of paradox, and the *reverse language* according to the Lakota Sioux tradition. This *Rite of Passage* I will discuss at length in another chapter but my intention here is to give some context for what I wanted to share in terms of symbols and metaphors.

Deprivation is the benediction of excess. That was part of the reason I was out here—to take a brutally honest look at my excessive use of alcohol and self-inflation that was propping me up as *"His Majesty."*

It is amazing how much discomfort one experiences when there is no refuge from the creepy-crawlies, mosquitos, and chiggers that are a large part of family when you are fortunate enough to find a sandbar upon a river that is ever changing the land formations. The privilege of sitting on a chair with a straight back I have taken for granted for too long—not anymore!

It was about the third day of my fasting experience that I became exhausted, burned to a crisp from paddling for hours without a sandbar with any shade provided, and angry that I could not control my discomfort levels. To make things worse, the wind was blowing directly against me and I was not able to progress at all. In fact, I was getting blown into outlets and banks along the river. I could *see* the wind coming toward me as the ripples on the river increased and gave me cue to paddle hard to try and get ahead of that force preventing me from progressing. Each attempt to *"beat the wind"* resulted in exhaustion and failure. I do not remember how many times I tried out rowing the wind, but I do remember that it culminated by me yelling at God and cursing him for not helping me, and for making my life so *"miserable"*!

The magical metaphor rose out of the breath of my Creator by blowing my canoe in a circle as if I was on a carousel. I threw my paddle down into the canoe knowing I was beat and that surrendering to a force greater than myself was the only move left for me. I was *spent*, like an *empty cartridge*; I had no *propellant* left to *ignite any resolve*. Exhausted from rowing, sun scorched, and no food in my belly for four days I had had enough, yet there was no way out. I was here in this *naked* moment of *"now"* and I could not change my circumstances. I could only yield myself to this sacred time. I began to weep bitterly. Dehydration had not stolen my tears from me; *they came like a waterfall.* My eyes filled to the extent of not being able to see, only feel. Here I am going around and around in a circle, weeping bitterly, blinded by my own tears, exhausted and angry. Can you picture this?

When I had yelled myself to hoarseness and had expelled all my energy in a final collapse, the voice of my Creator spoke to me, and gave my heart the understanding of all that was happening. Funny that when silence and surrender meet, God's voice becomes very clear and so easy to hear. This was my *takeaway* from the intuitive voice of God:

"DAKOTA, HOW IS THIS LIKE YOUR LIFE? HOW DO YOU ROW AGAINST THE WORLD IN YOUR LIVING? IS IT REALLY ME YOU ARE ANGRY AT, OR ARE YOU ANGRY AT YOURSELF BECAUSE OF YOUR

PREVIOUS CHOICES? HOW ARE YOU 'SPINNING YOUR WHEELS' AND GOING AROUND IN CIRCLES IN GENERALITY, WITH LITTLE SPECIFICITY? HOW DO YOU ROW AGAINST ME?"

When I arrived home, I looked at my life much differently. I saw the blessing of a chair and for the first time in my life sat consciously with gratitude for its remarkable design. All the mundane things in my life I had taken for granted were *recreated blessings*. Taking a shower was no longer an inconvenience. *To be clean and feel clean is now a holy experience.*

I was ravenously hungry to sit in these questions and discern for myself the authentic answers to them, and I have. Taking inventory on this insight given me is a way to examine my honesty.

The Bible says in the book of Nahum that *God's way is in the whirlwind and storm, and the clouds are the dust of his feet.* After this personal experience, those words of scripture are more than metaphor and description; they are *active* and true. *My storm* endured in that canoe became a *living pathway*, leading me to greater radiance throughout my future on Earth, teaching me also that *paradox is the promised land* available to all who are willing to make pilgrimage to it. *It is obvious Blessing* and *Curse* do exist together. Many more examples could be shared in terms of symbol and metaphor but a glimpse much like an *appetizer*, sometimes satisfies hunger in a better way than a full *buffet* because it's all that's needed.

I do wish to share one more living metaphor that was a profound insight for helping me to see myself through the lens of mystical knowing:

How I am like a cauldron of boiling rice:

Transformation does not occur without some type of process. This usually involves *time, temperature,* and *tension.* While boiling water the other day in preparation to make a pot of brown rice, I was struck with the parallel of my personal transformation of being *"cooked"* much the same way as the rice was being cooked just right for my personal and public consumption.

The *pot* or *cauldron* represented my body as the *"container,"* my flesh outfit. The *water* within the cauldron represented my *spirit* and *psyche.* The *rice* represented my personality and ego, the little "I" *within.* The burner of course was the *working,* or *heat of the Great Mystery,* the unknown part of transcendence that does what it does. Finally, the *covering or lid* for that pot was represented as *my covering* for my *belief systems* and ironically the lid was glass, so that spoke to me also regarding *transparency.* Needless to state here, there was symbolism galore to work with, much the same as occurs during dreamtime.

Boiling water began to move the hard kernels of rice in a fountain of taupe colored foam. Instantly *I began to see the process of transforming energy that takes place within me, otherwise unseen, but through experiential means.*

When the *hardened part of me is boiled away* by the process of *time, temperature,* and *tension, it is then that I may become a blessing of transformative power or knowing with which I can feed those who are hungry enough to partake in what morsels I joyfully offer.*

Tenderness only occurs after the *transformative energy of heat.* It is then that my heart is receptive to mysteries calling and purified enough to have the truest and authentic empathy for all that lives and breathes.

The *steam* on the glass lid *reminds me to always be transparent,* even when much is at risk, for my *vulnerability creates a safer place for those near me who are in fear.*

The beads of water on the inside of the lid are my *tears* I hold in, that eventually must be released and dried through the new life perspective given me through the *"boiling."*

The scars on the cauldron are my *badges of honor* that I cannot hide from those who choose to *"see"* me. *My scars are my greatest gift* because they have taught me that I am able to withstand the *heat* of unknown outcomes, that results in knowing myself better and integrating the lessons learned along the way. "Oops, I think my rice is boiling!"

We have travelled far together in this chapter. We have traversed the *landscape* of the *mundane* and *extraordinary* by looking at symbols and metaphors as written and living expressions. We have defined both in two separate realms. For me, the question of sacred or secular isn't as important to ask as it is to ask myself: *"Am I integrating the message and medicine I've been given through transcendence?"* Your answer may be completely different. That's the whole point! Finding first this seemingly hidden treasure, then applying it for our own edification and efficacy for living, which then enables us to live out of *bliss* rather than *mundanity*. Like the symbols and metaphors often given us during dreamtime, we can now embrace with confidence and knowing, that *"magic"* is real and all around us in the natural world *speaking* to us this way.

Abraham Maslow developed a theory called Hierarchy of Needs. This theory contains five levels of needs. He explains lower level needs must be met before we are concerned with the higher level of needs. In order of lowest to highest, they are the following: (1) Physiological, (2) Safety, (3) Social, (4) Self-Esteem, and (5) Self-Actualization.

When our *being* is filled in an environment we can feel relaxed and safe, with relative good health and encouragement to be who we are by friendships and family, we are then properly equipped to *treasure hunt* in the fourth and fifth levels of Maslow's theory to gain greater insight. It is within the fourth and fifth levels of Maslow's theory that we can discover who we are, and for developing into the *one who walks beside us that we are too often not.* If indeed we have met the first three levels of the Hierarchy of Needs, then we have no excuse not to pursue the fourth and fifth levels, right? *What is at risk if you don't? What is at risk if you do?* The answer to those questions will reveal much about your approach to living and perhaps reveal a *shadow* that needs facing. *Could it be fear of the unknown?*

I wish to conclude by saying this:

In the first three levels in the *Hierarchy of Needs* we have the personal perspective of the ordinary and mundane being met. We can see them as the "youth" of our growing experience, important but somewhat rudimentary, basic but also necessary. The last two levels of hierarchal needs are about the *magic*—the *reclaiming*, the *severing* of what is unwanted, and *rewriting* my story and telling it the way I wish. The freedom of discovering for the first time without influence, my personal allegory. Not following a design or pattern that some people necessarily understand, but discovering for ourselves, and claiming unabashed, our *right to be who we are*—unique and mysterious, profound yet foolish at times. Enlightened yet ignorant. Interpreting life through a lens that we alone grind for the world vision we see through our own understanding, and not edited by those who think they know better because they hold a PhD.

I am not attacking men and women who have applied the discipline of learning. What I am saying is that *who knows better than me* who I am and *who I am becoming? Who knows better than me that I am the heroes I admire, and the people I hate?* It is my work and privilege to find this out for myself. Richard Rohr writes in his book, *Seeing Like a Mystic*, **"If we do not mythologize our living, we will pathologize it."** That has become a risk I do not wish to take. I'm well acquainted with the pathology of living; there is more at risk for me by not diving head first into the realm of symbols and metaphor. There is more at risk for me *by not looking for God in places that I think HE/SHE would not be.* The search has become *spiritual artistry* as a spiritual artist and enabling myself to come closer to mastering the art of *living my bliss.* I have many miles ahead, but I'm having a ball. I hope now you can too, if indeed you are not already!

The Glory That Is Woman

She is the inspiration and substance of my sacred dreamtime.

She is the radiant beacon that fuels my ever-flourishing heart, yet the *shadow* that shades me from the scorch of the passionate Sun.

She whispers soft and tender words from her eyes that speak.

She believes in me when I find it difficult to believe in myself.

She is often the *poetry of my thought,* the *melody I harmonize with,* and *the beginning that has no end.*

She is the *paragon* of all creatures . . .

She wakes in the *masculine radiance,* and I recede in the *feminine cool glow* of *moonlit dreamtime.*

Covenant with my wife was born in the phase of the waxing moon. I am struck with the epiphany that I have married the *Sun*, and she the *Moon*. Together we seem to have unconsciously constellated the androgynous paradox of two living as one.

In our imperfection we are blessed perfectly with one another. God's pleasure is the smile we share with one another.

I am a man who has been redeemed by the wholeness of unconditional love. I have lived long enough to know the fullness and wholeness of love through the woman that amazingly said "YES" to me. It is in this spirit that I author these lines of honoring and dedication.

What are the roles that women have had in your life? Looking backward at your life, were there any pivotal moments where the female brought power, or some other gift to your living? Do you view women as equal to men in design, or do they bring larger or lesser amounts of what you as a man wish to emanate? Is there any healing that needs to occur in your relationship with women?

I want to extol the positive roles that women have played throughout my life and give homage to their positive affecting of my evolution as a man. *Without the blessing of the female spirit, none of us would be here today.*

I wish to give tribute to women as "the *Sacred Life Givers*," "*Affecters of Dreams*," and "*Soulmates*."

As the *Sacred Life Givers*, women give all men their existence through the pain of childbearing and the nurturing of their breast. There are other ways that they give life that we will discuss later.

As the *Affecters of Dreams,* nothing makes a mother or wife prouder than to see a husband, son, or daughter flourish in their chosen pathways. Many times it is the encouragement of the woman that helps sustain the vision and dreams that men hold for their living.

As *Soulmates,* the perfect androgyne is formulated by balancing male and female energies and essence in perfect proportions. This bond creates the mystical paradox of *two becoming one.*

This is an appropriate and fitting summation from Myles Munroe Inspiration, *Knowing the Woman*:

Females are incubators. God made them that way, which is why whatever you give to a woman, she multiplies it and gives it back to you.

If you give a woman sperm, she multiplies it, gives it life, and gives you a baby. You give her a house, she multiplies it and gives you a home. You give her groceries, she multiplies that and gives you a meal. You give her a word, she multiplies it and gives you a sentence. You give her frustration, multiply that and she'll give you hell.

You can always tell what you've given a woman by what she's given back to you.

This summation though not comprehensive by any means, gives strong evidence and example that women have innately mastered the Laws of Multiplicity and are formidable in their resolve for affecting the circle and *sacred hoop* of life.

Among the burdens women as the *sacred life givers* carry is the *powerlessness* they must accept in bringing new life into the world. I am struck by the tremendous strength women exemplify during their pregnancy—the hormonal changes and the tummy increasing in size. Yet when at work, the glow of motherhood seems to sustain an inner joy amongst the added weight, worry, and concern for bringing a healthy life into a world of ever-increasing turmoil. *Being honest, if it were me carrying a child, I would most likely be wearing a crinkled brow, amplified by a frown, and blaming "woman" just as Adam did for my beguilement!*

Motherhood does not allow the privilege of *special ordering* all the features desired in the new life growing within her; rather, it is the acceptance of an unknown outcome.

As the *sacred life givers*, single or plural, it seems intrinsic that motherhood instills a *"whatever it takes" warrior* mentality for affecting their offspring. There are always exceptions to any rule, however I applaud and honor those strengths in women that I have personally witnessed.

When my mother brought me into the world, she had no way of knowing how many times I would disappoint her or make her proud. Despite choices made by their offspring, Mothers must carry the burden of accepting outcomes that continuously break their heart, or the success that draws their sons or daughters further away from them for sake of career, or commitment to themselves for building their own *King* or Queendoms.

Women as Sacred Life Givers are bridled with both blessing and curse. It takes a very strong character to remain whole and positive when the yielding of both success and failure brings the same feeling of separation and sense of loss.

Just as cutting the umbilical cord after birth brings symbolic and physical separation, so the strength of the woman during Motherhood must allow her to sever the ties to the boy, so that he can return home a man, and conversely the daughter. Though this is a necessary part of the Mother/ Son/ Daughter evolution, it doesn't necessarily make it pleasant for either one. *Women as Sacred Life Givers* understand the importance of severing and letting go for the sake of their offspring to flourish.

Why is it that some women see the gold in their men, that men cannot see in themselves?

Among the glory that makes women who they are is their loyalty to the way they love. Tenacious in their love, women will endure for years the *shadows* of men that men themselves often refuse to face. It gives strong evidence that perhaps *women in some cases are better at being women, than men are at being men!*

During a night of binge drinking and the world throwing its dung at me, I arrived on the doorstep of my dance partner who is now my wife. Bloodied, disheveled, and spiritually bankrupt, I arrived with nothing to offer her but a tortured soul. She had every reason on earth to turn me away, but because the well of her love for me ran so deep, she instead invited me in. What she did to this very day still astonishes me and makes my heart tender.

In a gesture of Christ-like comfort, she put towels on her living room floor and began washing my naked shame from me. The splashing sound of water droplets being wrung from the cleansing cloth amplified my internal loneliness while the tender touch of warm water and loving service gave companionship to the emptiness that was my heart. Her loving kindness became my *stay of execution* and I slept that night in the safety and comfort of an angel of mercy who made a conscious choice of looking only at the gold in me, that I had no faith for believing existed. Loving me to greater wholeness is the special anointing my wife held for me before she became my wife. It's a wonderment for me that after all the tumult and dark nights of soul, she never gave up on me. Twenty-four years passed before a covenant could occur. She waited! Her tenacity in loving, and vision for seeing the man beneath the veils, was the greatest *gift of life* that I have ever received. I cannot say for sure, but I am skeptical that there could be any greater example in my lifetime of *"the laying down of life for another"* my wife gave to me during the many moons of my personal *Shadow Dance*. Perhaps another main topic should have been added . . . "Women as Miracle Workers"!

Pursuing my passion to dance while living in a small farming community wasn't met with great enthusiasm by many, in fact, very few, including both my parents.

There was, however, the mother of a former girlfriend (Sharon) who shared my dream and vision of bringing social dance to my community. I remember sitting at their kitchen table, her patience and mutual enthusiasm for helping in the creation of structure, cost, and venue for my private enterprise. She seemed genuinely interested in my success and encouraged me greatly by her help.

I did manage to attract a few lessons from willing participants, but it became clear that I was not a good fit for my hometown. Sharon's gift to me however was in the support and personal affecting of my vision for dance. This was a seed that bore over time one of the longest running ballroom dance schools in Madison, Wis., and some of the top ballroom dancers in the nation! *Could it be that women relate to men's dreams so well because they honor the right-brain of intuition and dreamtime more aptly?*

My wife and I met through a dance audition and worked together in the same franchise. Hoping to expand our knowledge and financial opportunity, we moved to Phoenix, Ariz. Excelling at work there was not in direct proportion to wage earning, and we had hoped to buy a house, compete in dancing, and live happily ever after. It was not meant to be, and I began to question my choice of profession.

After agonizing over whether I should find a different profession, it occurred to me that we may have outgrown the franchise that gave birth to our career. *One must leave the parent to flourish on one's own terms!*

Within two weeks' time, we were headed back to Madison, Wis. to fulfill our destiny as studio owners. We had no money and no business plan, but we were filled with excitement and hope. *We had burned our ship* and there could be no turning back. I knew innately that I had what it takes to be successful at operating a studio. The ingredient that was most important in manifesting that mutual dream was how, without any guarantee, my partner stood with me and together we recreated our career in dance and built on our own a very successful studio with twenty-seven years of operation. When men are supported by the women they love, limitation does not exist, and they begin building temples for their goddess. This is an indisputable truth that has unfolded for me. The glory that is *Woman as Affecter of Dreams* is arriving home on a credit card with no guarantee of success but trusting in the process of life and in the vision of her man's desire. After this example I have had to ask myself, *"If this was in reverse, would you have stood as firmly by her side"?* My honesty renders the answer, *"I highly doubt it."* If I did, it would have been begrudgingly. Sometimes it hurts being honest, especially when the portrait image on the canvas doesn't match the living example. There is a gift to receive in knowing that: The gift is to no longer waste time in *canvass portrayal* of image, but *authentic "showing up"* and being ever vigilant of my personal self-absorption with my relationship. *Woman as Affecter* has taught me that on and off the dance floor of life.

Giving examples of *Woman as the Sacred Giver of Life* and *Affecter of Dreams* is an honoring due to many women known and unknown to me. I am now going to discuss the *Woman as Soulmate.*

We have been told that the divorce rate in America is at 50 percent. Latest statistics according to the American Psychological Association state that it is somewhere between 40-50 percent and that subsequent marriages are even higher. According to Refinery 29, the divorce rate peaked at 40 percent and it is declining. The consensus is that there is no fixed number that accurately pinpoints the divorce rate because divorce and marriage rates vary drastically in different groups of people.

Here is the point I wish to make regarding the data shared: *Do these statistics reflect our inability to choose our mates well or has time, temperature, and tension taken its toll on the relational evolution?"*

Isn't Covenant supposed to be the spiritual container that constellates the axis mundi during times of turmoil? If so, then what's going on?

Relationships are as complex as the people involved in them. Certainly, there are circumstances that test the strength in any relationship: betrayal, substance abuse, economics. The list is endless. *What causes the split in some while others remain?*

Remaining or departing from a relationship is highly personal, and consequences of either choice will occur. Understanding the "how" in arrival to a destination sometimes is made easier by looking at its original departure.

Most people ending up divorced that I have known state that, before they got married, they knew deep within themselves that it was not a consecration that should have taken place. Many of those I have talked to have given clear evidence as indicators for refrain yet made a conscious choice to ignore those explicit indications. Deep in their gut they knew they were settling for a counterfeit of covenantal bliss. This is a very common backdrop for too many couples who have suffered failed marriages. I feel great sadness for those folks, some of whom are family and longtime friends. I hold a certain amount of anger in a general sense for both parties getting cheated out of their Divine experience of creating the sacred androgyne and having a life mate forever to explore life's mysteries.

Men and women get married for many different reasons: tax deductions, pregnancy, convenience, good looks, or spontaneity. When a man or woman marries their soulmate, however, the covenant has been ordained and consecrated long before the ceremony takes place, and both parties know and experience that fact together simultaneously.

Marriage signifies a mature moving on; there is the temptation to rush down the highway of life just to prove our ability to get somewhere. That arrival may not be where you belong, however. Woman as Soulmate unfolds herself in *Kairos* time, not *Chronos* time, which is like the sacred birth of a son or daughter. A *Soulmate* appears as a gift from the Great Mystery and liminality of the *outer space of inner desire. You have nothing to do with its arrival. Essence and emanations are the invisible ingredients that create a soul tie that personality, wealth, wit, or good looks can never manipulate.*

Soulmates are seldom in a hurry. They are the contented and silent observers who patiently wait for the *"true coming"* to unfold. They suffer joyfully in the sorrows of the world and accept the strife, dissension, and discord as the immaturity of love expressing its youthful ignorance. Woman as Soulmate is the combination of Mother wisdom and vibrant youth, waiting to leap into the open arms of her long waited for eternal *lover.*

Woman as Soulmate disciplines her love giving for only those skilled in loving themselves first. *She does not demand the best from her mate; she seduces him into providing it.* She actuates what is inactive simply by being actively calm, yet calmly active. She has made industriousness into a fine art.

Woman as Soulmate is an ever-healing presence, a most formidable *Warrior*, Resourceful Magician, Royal in resolve, and sublimely splendid as *Lover*. Nothing is the equal on earth as the arrival of Woman as Soulmate. She is the blessing to be searched for yet waited on in the same way a rose is not given until after it has bloomed.

I have invited, perhaps, the accusation of *confirmation bias* to my limited portrayal of women during this chapter—a *viewpoint from rose colored glasses*. I wish to remind the reader that my intention was to speak only of the gold I have witnessed in women and that volumes more could be offered. Of course, all women, like men, have their uninte-grated *shadows*.

If I see a *bitch, ballbuster, slut,* or *airhead*, what I don't see is a woman wounded somewhere along the road of life in their *archetypal hardwiring*. It might be true that the *slut* seldom felt loved as a child and is compensating through artificial intimacy.

It may be true that the *bitch* in youth was not allowed her own private boundaries and in the interest of protecting herself keeps the best intentions at bay.

It might be true that the *ballbuster* was subject to a dominating presence that did not allow her *inner alpha* to choose for herself the way to shine and has very little toler-ance for anyone not allowing her to be *Her*.

The *airhead* may be putting off making clear choices for herself because every choice she made as a youth was criticized or wrong. Keeping her options always open is a way to avoid criticism or being wrong.

Remember that we tend to see the world the way we are and not the way the world truly is! Keeping this in mind is a good way of *seeing with the eyes of your heart,* I believe.

Seeing women in their golden qualities of *Sacred Life Giver, Affecter of Men's Dreams,* and *Soulmate* highlights the relevance and viability of women as equal yet unique contributors as worldbuilders, and worldbuilding. If I see women at all, them I must see everything they are and not allow myself to identify with labels and my own *confirmation of bias.*

I have been given a start in this world by knowing *Woman as Sacred Life Giver.* I have lived a private dream and career through knowing *Women as Affecter of Men's Dreams.* With Woman as *Soulmate,* I have been given the mythological *"Heaven on Earth"* as manifest reality—the greatest gift given me totally undeserved. God must have wanted me to know what is true love. My values, attitudes, and beliefs concerning love have been completely shattered and reformulated because true love redefines the lofty and gooey notion of romanticized intimacy.

As a heterosexual man living in a diverse world, my take-away from the modeling of women is that a part of me is in them, and a part of them is in me. It is the realization of *"WE"* more than *"I"* or *"YOU."* It has become the sacred *"US."*

Collectively, we are the higher and lower versions of one another during *progress* and *regress.* "WE" are vanishing bit by bit, day by day. There is a sense of urgency to make amends somehow for what I could have been to women in earlier days but somehow was not. Design does not allow going back to the *Garden* for a do-over; however, it does allow consciousness to awaken out of the misty sleep of limited perceptions.

Knowing this, the very best I will be able to do moving forward is to love all women through my wife, seeing them with the eyes of my heart, and being ever mindful that what I see in them is also a part of me.

"Boons" We Offer the World

All men and women, great in accomplishment or not, leave a legacy of themselves in the wake of their lives. *From the date of our birth to the date of our passing have you ever wondered what the hyphen between those two dates will contain?*

As a younger man I never gave any thought to the idea of legacy or worldbuilding of any type. I was in the *Warrior Energy* of building an existence for myself through vocation and social circle. As the *Aging Elder,* that outlook has changed profoundly. Participating as joyfully as I can in the sorrows of the world has given me great pause to ponder how I may affect my world around me with some positive contribution.

Here is a challenge for you: write down the date of your birth, put a hyphen after it, and then a question mark, 1958 to? Now, fill in the hyphen with what you would want the world to benefit from based on your living experience. *What is it that you value that you would want the world to embrace for higher living?* "He came to serve, not to be served," might replace or be the synonym to that hyphen. That is the legacy left to the world as a modeling of selfless service and humble living. *How would the world not benefit from that exemplative example?*

I wish to share my viewpoint and perspectives on the *"hyphen"* of our life paths. The genesis of life is mostly about constructing that life—finding our niche, social circle, and vocations. This is the *Warrior* finding the way that works for them or sustains them. Following the *Warrior* way of personal world building is the *Lover Energy* opening the heart to relationships and perhaps *settling down* with the object of desire found through exclusivity of a mate. *Magician Energy* inflates through processing the necessities of raising a family or remaining a *"singular plural."* This may contain the rethinking of priorities in terms of social, economic, and personal needs for a viable home structure. The last stage of life appears in the *Royal quadrant* which is concerned with overall blessing for a flourishing kingdom or family unit, and the *legacy* and strong *Eldership* for progeny and future generations. As we age, the questions we are left with are: *"What gifts do I bring into the world, and what shall be the legacy that I leave behind? Will it be monetary inheritance only, or is there a greater boon that I may offer the world before my passing?"*

I wish to fill in the remainder of the hyphen with these four life aspects that speak to the ending point and date of our passing before it becomes the stone monument that is etched with our epitaph. These are: *Recognizing our gifts to offer, Elderhood* and *wisdom, Modeling wisdom and maturity,* Leaving *a* legacy of *those boons to our progeny and future generations.*

Eldership is the outward expression of revealing to the youth of community, the *inner gold* mined from personal wisdom and experience gained during the earlier stages of living. Most of us are well acquainted with uncles, aunts, grandmothers, and grandfathers as the *Elder* figures in our lives. Elder*s* and *Eldership* comes in the form of mentoring on behalf of someone who needs positive affecting and guidance. There is no requirement of being a blood relative for being an *Elder*. *Eldership* is the action of freely giving from compassion and benefit as helpmate to those who may need it. It is a loving *sponsorship* that has no contract other than "*standing with.*" My judgement is that good *Eldership* is becoming a scarce commodity today, yet it remains one of the last hopes of modeling being our *brother's keeper*, and for displaying the *Royal Energy* of centering, holding a vision to fruition, fostering, affecting, and blessing agent. *Elders*, both men and women, are compositions of lifetime's accumulated knowledge actuated into wisdom by applying what they have learned. Passing that accumulated wisdom onto younger generations through the motive of *affecting positively* is why *Elders* and *Eldership* are a resource "*We the People*" should not neglect.

How does one recognize and acquire the gifts or boons they wish to share with the world?

Life experience and copious amounts of self-reflection are staples within the *Elder Community*. The *regression* of aging brings the *progression* of what we wish to pass on either to family, friends, or the world at large.

It is a natural process to look backwards at life as an *Elder* because we are very aware that mortality's chapter is waiting to be written. Looking backwards at the wealth of life experience becomes another natural process of *editing* the living experience into parts of what has been useful, and what has been misspent in youthful indulgences. We begin to recognize yet another shift in our value systems and delineate what we believe holds the greatest value for us.

We acquire our *gifts* and *boons* to offer through the process of our living. We begin to recognize that money buys a lot of distractions but not necessarily lasting happiness. Simply put, the *boons* and *gifts* that come to us appear from the process of experiencing Dante's *Inferno*: "*Abandon all hope ye who enter here*"—*going through hell* while building a life and understanding in metaphorical terms "*being in the belly of the whale.*" These *past curses* become the *future blessings* for others when *Eldership* is modeled. The talents we are born with and utilize in our living will never be superseded by life experience. Men and women do not become wise overnight. It is the process of *time, tension,* and *temperature* that formulates the wisdom to be passed on later to *those who have the ears to hear!*

It isn't difficult to recognize a qualified Elder. *Great Eldership* is embodied by the axiom: **"Good humored patience is necessary with mischievous children and your own mind"** (Robert Aitkin Roshi).

True Elders are well acquainted with Walter Scott's famous quotation, **"Oh what a tangled web we weave, when first we practice to deceive."** *True Elders* know that the first lie perpetuates into a lifestyle of lying, and, beyond that, Elderhood reveals through experience that it is ourselves we deceive the most. The *True Elder* demonstrates the ability to laugh at himself for his folly and *shadow* expressions. Shame and guilt are not within the tool bag of an able *Elder* for they know that shame and guilt tear down the human soul; they are only invested in building up. *Good Eldership* is a gentle leading for inexperience to own its *shadow* behaviors, because the high cost is never discovering nor enjoying *personal bliss*. *Eldership* models the aging process with childlike wonder, tranquility, and a willingness to be comfortable in imperfection. The wisdom of *Elderhood* teaches the inexperience of youth that perfectionism is grandiosity, the more you look at something, the more you see it, and that developing a *cadence* in life yields greater opportunity for seeing what others have missed. Please feel free to add any qualities for formulating *Eldership* that I may not have mentioned.

I have given my ideal of what an Elder should embody. How they have received and learned to recognize their boons to give the world qualifies them as the *wise sage* that spares inexperience and youth unnecessary suffering and pain, *if* they have *ears to hear* their impartations. I wish now to share wisdom that I have gleaned from those whom I hold great respect for and who have stood with me in some way during my life process. I asked them similar questions as in the beginning of this chapter: *"What is it that you value, that you would want the world to embrace for higher living?" "What would you want the world to know before you pass on?"*

Self-reflection and life experience drawn from the wellspring of inner brilliance have inspired these people to share their *boons*:

Roger Rafferty, who is a retired Marine and Viet Nam Vet, has this to say: ***"Don't be afraid to grow old; too many that I have known never had that privilege."***

Royce La Liberty, who is a friend, has this to say: ***"Approach each day with a little humor!"***

Terry Kringle, who is a retired educator, has this to say: ***"Find a partner to share your life with who accepts the whole you."*** And this also: ***"Begin saving now for your*** *future. Even a small amount, weekly or monthly, can grow to a tidy sum over a long period of time."*

Charles Engel, retired MD, has this to say: *"Always be honest with yourself and with your dealings with others."*

Lee Petz, who is a professional bodybuilder and training expert, has this to say: *"Our purest place lies not in the reverence of knowledge, belief, or status. Rather, it is the humble nature of wonder that makes us capable of truly being wonderful."*

Gwen Engel, who is a retired RN and professional dance teacher and former studio owner, has this to say: *"Learn to be self-reliant, solve your own problems, but have the wisdom to seek help when you need it."*

Malachite Windancer, who is the four-legged *daughter* we will never have, models this behavior: *"Make yourself available; opportunity is everywhere for you to get what you want."*

Kenneth Burg, who is a psychiatrist, has this to say: *"Be courageous in support of equality for women."*

Diana Engel, who is a Nutritionist and homemaker, has this to say: *"Set goals as a young person and work to follow those goals to establish direction in life."*

Steven Vedro, a Ritual Elder for the ManKind Project, has this to say: *"All that we do in life connects to the past and future reality. Healing in this lifetime changes not just the future, but also the past."*

Julie Cloutier Rocha, who is a retired CPA, has this to say: *"Follow your passion and do not allow discouragement from others to keep you from believing in yourself."*

Max Weber, a Ritual Elder for the ManKind Project, has this to say: *"It is better to be interested than interesting." "If you recognize that it's All About You, it is easier to quiet the inner voice that is telling you it is All About Them."*

Megann Lawry, a friend, has this to say: *"You will always have regrets. Face them, accept them, make peace with them. Don't let them tear you up."*

Mark Burke, a retired law enforcement official, has this to say: *"When you look at someone and are intrigued by them, not exclusively by physical demeanor, get to know them. If they have something you want, find out through them how they achieved what seems so shiny to you."*

Patti Puccio, administrative assistant, has this to say: *"Bring passion to whatever it is that you do. Work ethic must contain a bounty of faithfulness, honesty, loyalty, and love. These attributes signify the best you can do."*

Gary Moseson, who is a retired psychotherapist, has this to say: *"As adults, it is useful for each of us to remind ourselves that 'I' am no longer a wounded child. I am solid, like a mountain. From this centered and grown-up awareness, we can find great meaning, joy, and connection by living a life of generosity and compassion."*

John Norman, who is a retired agricultural science professor, has this to say: *"We are much more than we think, more amazing, powerful, and mysterious than our minds can comprehend. To live fulfilled, I search the desire of my heart, the center of my being, my essence, and be the Love that I AM."*

And as one simmers within the questions of their living, *"What is beyond what is seen, and what is within us that lies latent waiting* for *its voice to be heard?* Realization occurs that we are exactly as the external mystery: *Our darkness blinds us, and our radiance sometimes causes others to shield their eyes or turn away. We must reconcile the extremes of night and day by finding respite in the shadow. Every day and every night, then, is a reminder and a metaphor of who we are, and of how we become. Eldership is the application of constant becoming for eternal being.*

There can be no question now that the process of our lives formulates the boons we have to offer. *Child-like innocence and wonder provide the magic elixir the world doesn't know it needs.*

Receiving our gifts comes from the life process of *mountain top summiting,* or through *Dante's hell.* It is the substance of our living that make up the *hyphen* chiseled on stone before death.

Eldership becomes a civic duty and an unceremonious event for mentorship and generativity on the behalf of those who need and are willing to climb the ladder for finding their *bliss.*

Elders are playing the role of *King* Arthur's *Merlin* through their individual and unique modeling of *holding the center* and application of their wisdom in living.

Lastly, through grace and a nobility that only the aging process can provide, the Elder awards their *boons* as a legacy. Before passing on, one final gift-giving occurs. The gift or *boon,* which is part of legacy, is the value held in a lifetime of joyfully or painfully suffering in the sorrows of the world.

My Elder's heart wills these *boons* to the world and what I would want them to know:

"Live in the knowing that you are more than you think you are, accomplishing more than you think you can. The difficulty of being is in the constant becoming, this becoming itself is prodigious."

"Belief systems keep one safe for a while. Sooner or later a shattering occurs that destroys everything you thought to be certain. Wisdom is the willingness to evolve."

"Oxymoron becomes a verb of living, and the noun of paradox becomes the promised land of metaphysical wonderment."

"Honor your belly's fire; it will lead you into the mastery of working and playing at the same time and a successful career of finding and living your bliss."

"Don't be afraid to shine; give reverence for how often."

My final boon to offer the sons and daughters of the future generations is reflected through my Father's heart:

If I Were Your Father

If I were your Father, I would tell you that my plans for you are to watch you shine in your growing.

If I were your Father, I would tell you that failure is the negative way of looking at growth.

If I were your Father, I would tell you that we are called to a Hero's journey. Refusing the call only prolongs the process of personal self-discovery and our gifts to share within the world community.

If I were your Father, I would tell you to explore the functionality of all your feelings. Too many men and women feel only with lonely genitals.

If I were your Father, I would tell you that as a woman, you are a sacred life giver, and as a man, you are the guardian of sacred life.

If I were your Father, I would tell you that dream's and imagination are the components that sustain your life; a college degree is resume material. Each are beneficial; only one leads to a career. You must decide which . . . but integrate both.

If I were your Father, I would tell you that our mutual soul tie means that there never has to be any withholding between us. Nothing is inexpressible, nothing is off limits.

If I were your Father, I would tell you to let go of the life I have planned for you, so that you may discover for yourself the one that is waiting.

If I were your Father, I would tell you that my expression of love toward you may seem twisted at times. Be patient with me in my decline, as I have been patient during you're ascension. Aging isn't always kind.

If I were your Father, I would tell you to make good choices for yourself not following the crowd but staying true to yourself. I will stand with you during the pain of isolated truth.

If I were your Father, I would tell you that the world will tempt you with promises and illusions of satisfaction and fulfillment, but that you are the only one who can supply that for yourself by balanced living and doing that which is right.

If I were your Father, I would tell you that you will do well to mythologize your living by dreaming big and ritualiz-

ing your joy and pain, and that it is worth the effort, though the outcome is unknown.

If I were your Father, I would tell you that your loving is reflected through your living. You cannot expect to get what you have not discovered in yourself.

If I were your Father, I would tell you that we are all defined by three words: WE ARE LOVED. Creator makes us within the paradox of same, yet unique.

If I were your Father, I would tell you that I will love you whether you are white, red, yellow, or any other color of the rainbow. I will love you whether you are gay, hetero, or asexual. I will learn from my love for you how to honor your sacred space and direction.

If I were your Father, I would tell you that I know what I know through experience, not just from books. My best mentoring has come through the sacred fires of seeking my truth. I bless your effort.

If I were your Father, I would tell you that the world is unjust at times. Placing blame is living in the powerlessness of victimhood, but by living the greatest version of yourself, you subdue all obstruction that keeps you from your bliss.

If I were your Father, I would tell you that finding and living your bliss inspires others to do the same. Great leadership rises from great example.

If I were your Father, I would tell you to try very hard not to judge others. You don't know what they are going through, what they've been through, or the lack of support they have had to arrive where they are. Understanding this creates empathy and perhaps a future alliance when it is needed the most.

If I were your Father, I would tell you to never stop learning about yourself. Who you are today does not define you tomorrow or years from now.

If I were your Father, I would tell you not to be deceitful or selfish in your relations with women. Your behavior toward them dictates their behavior toward you, but it speaks volumes as to the type of man you are.

If I were your Father, I would tell you to be more discerning of yourself before choosing a mate. The choice you make will affect you forever. It is wise for men and women to allow true love its natural unfolding.

Lastly, if I were your Father, I would tell you that when my time of passing comes . . . celebrate my living experience by remembering that I took claim over my lifepath on my own terms. I lived in the joy of working and playing simultaneously and was fortunate more than most to have found true love before my exit. Celebrate the way I chose to live and be happy for me that my rest is like the Sun at winter. I will shine from a greater distance in my hiding from you. Miss me only a little . . .

What are the boons you would offer to this list? There is the wonderful possibility that any of these offerings could become the spark needed for someone meeting their *greatest destiny* and *personal bliss.*

We plant the seed that we may not be allowed to harvest. As the planter, we must pass on, but our joy is made complete in the knowing that fruit from our seed sustains life for someone known, or someone never met. Our legacy never dies; it's passed on because our best is always recognized by others. That becomes ingredients for a future *boon* in the cycle and circle of life. Live well, that others may live . . .

Conclusion and Summary

"When Alexander saw the breadth of his domain, he wept for there were no more worlds left to conquer."
—Plutarch (c. 46–c. 125 AD).

Some scholars argue that Alexander wept not because there were no more worlds to conquer, but too little time to accomplish it.

In my youth, I set out to conquer the world in my own way. I believed that the world was for the taking, that I was bulletproof, and that the path to adventurous living would lead the way to my *"Golden Fleece."* Jason and the Argonauts had nothing on me!

Most of us have more than likely had our *world conquering* aspirations. Much like Alexander, we left the familiarity of home to conquer and world build through developing a career, finding a mate, and creating a social structure that supports our vision for living. Somehow along the way life presented itself in ways never anticipated, and the living experience lead to a *crucible.*

The point of this chapter is to remind and encourage you that you have all the tools required for emerging from that *crucible,* to *a greater life that awaits.*

A greater life awaits anyone who makes the choice to embody and integrate into their living any or all knowledge they have gleaned during the pilgrimage of *constant becoming.*

Magicians can know a thousand illusions and sleights of hands, but unless they personify the actual magic art by mesmerizing a crowd, their magic remains only mystical theory, never tested nor observed by others who may be inspired to *make disappear* that which is not needed.

A greater life awaits for anyone willing to evolve. I could be wrong, but it seems to me that we have the choice to either remain *stagnant* in complacency or *devolve* by darkened understanding or personal *ascension* through integrating the *shadows* of our living and embodying the *gold* of alchemical outcome. The choices we make, to move, or not to move, and how that moving occurs, is the reality we create for ourselves.

Attitudes, beliefs, and *values* are created from our *perception* of the world. Isn't it worth the time to thoroughly examine those components of living since so much is at stake for our future and progeny?

Since our lives are not *do-over dress rehearsals,* we have the right to empower ourselves to ineffable heights and abilities. One way of this self-empowering is through the integration of learning to *dance with our Shadow Partner.* Looking at our darkness with nighttime eyes, we learn not to fear the dark, and ironically, some of us find out that it was the power of our light we have feared, more than the darkness we were so familiar with.

Symbols and Metaphors became a way to interpret the natural world around us with a fresh and first-time eyes experience. Through the world of symbols and metaphors we realize our deep connection to every living thing. Fin, fur, feather, and flesh are merely the robes of a sacred beating heart and mutual divine breath.

Sacred and profane space opens the pathway for meeting with the Great Mystery and Transcendence. We are allowed the privilege of leaving the profane world of distraction, work, and illusion for the indescribable experience of *meeting ourselves* in the magical and mysterious Magnetic Center of Kairos time and through life-changing *Rites of Passage.*

Our Perception of reality has shifted by the integration occurring from the sacred space held during a *Rite of Passage.* We began the *excavation of our true self* that we know is a never-ending journey of regression and progression, disappointment and delight, with personal gifts for us in each circumstance. The many veils covering the truth we hid, denied, and repressed are being removed through this *spiritual dig.*

Muscarian Madness and the Peyote Religion gave the reader a glimpse at the folly and setbacks of *zeal without knowledge.* Wise men say only fools rush in; this is the lesson learned from the integration of this chapter. It is good to have passion, better yet to have the wisdom of restraint.

We learned and yet never too late that we can write our own chapter of Genesis through the *Origin and Resolution* story. We are placed in the world to write our own history, take on the Dragons of grandiosity, and kill them by becoming the greatest and mythological version of ourselves. We hold the keys to our greatest destiny through humility and self-reflection, with a bit of Transcendence being a part of the mixture.

For many of us the *apotheosis* and *zenith* of our living occurs the day we meet our soulmate through the *Glory that is Woman*. This chapter was meant to honor the sanctity of covenant and partner of life that helps to sustain our mutual existence and vision for living. Love is redefined, and loving thy neighbor as thyself becomes actualized doctrine for communal flourishing.

Through self-reflection during our elder years we sense the end of the world for ourselves and look backward at our living to see where we have been. It is within the silent reflection that our Elder heart opens and wishes to leave a *Boon we offer the World*. As Elders we have learned the folly of attachment to the world. We know too well that *we can't take it with us*, so we willingly bequeath all material goods to those whom we value. More than this, we have a great desire to leave a *boon* and legacy of spiritual wealth gleaned from the joy and pain of the Cosmic Crucible. It is our last act of love as we exchange the robe of flesh for cosmic light.

In conclusion, I would like to share these last thoughts with you:

Most of what I have written has taken place in the late hours of the night. It occurs to me that this is another metaphor I interpret as *gold* emerging from the *shadow*.

I am grateful for the process of my life. It wasn't very fun at times, but it is what I needed to get where I am now. I have learned that life is a paradox and trying to figure it out is like trying to empty the ocean with a pitchfork. There seems to be no vacuum in the realm of spirit; you reap what you sow, and I know that if I take myself too seriously, it's for sure nobody else will! A sense of humor is needed for establishing balance.

There will always be a grinding of will among the human family, but with these tools we can show up as *whole people* offering expression in a positive way and perhaps affecting others by example.

It is not after all what is *external* that causes my distress, it is what is *internal* that has yet to be resolved. This **is** the process of *coming together.* I think we can all agree that there is a great need for that now more than ever.

It is my sincere hope and wish that as people put upon this planet we can truly *see* each other and honor that we also only *see* in part.

We *see* the world the way we are, not the way it is. *A greater life awaits.*

Bibliography

Myles Munroe, Inspiration (1954–2014)

American Psychological Association (2017)

Refinery 29 (2017)

Signs and Symbols Sourcebook by Adele Nozedar (2010)

Holy Bible

Abraham Maslow, Hierarchy of Needs (1943)

Joseph Campbell, Reflections on the Art of Living, A Joseph Campbell Companion (1991, selected and edited by Diane K. Osbon)

King Warrior Magician Lover by Robert Moore (1990)

Men are from Mars, Women are from Venus by John Gray (1992)

The King Within by Robert Moore and Douglas Gillette (2010)

Gnostic Gospel of Thomas by Ron Miller (2004)

The Ancient Talmud

Return to Love by Marrianne Williamson (1992)

Nine Stages of Psychosocial Development by Erik Erikson (1959)

The Life Cycle Completed: Extended Version by Joan Erikson (1998)

The Wisdom of the Enneagram by Don Richard Riso and Russ Hudson (1999)

Positive Disintegration by Kazimierz Dabrowski (1902–1980)

Way of the Peaceful Warrior by Dan Millman (1980)

Cohen by Bill Moyers (1991)

The Hero with a Thousand Faces by Joseph Campbell (1949)
Johann Goethe (1814)
The Genius Myth by Michael Meade (2016)
The Seven Storey Mountain by Thomas Merton (1948)
Fire in the Belly by Sam Keen (1991)

About the Author

Dakota Windancer is a man of diverse background. He has acclaimed musical accomplishments and has produced two albums that are sold throughout the world. Dance, martial arts, and bodybuilding make up the other disciplines for which he has won regional and national acclaim. Windancer's personal journey to accomplishment and knowledge, which he gleaned along the way, are the prime motivation for writing this book. He attended college at the University of Wisconsin Madison as a choreography/performance major and has added to his bank of knowledge through the Earth medicines of sweat lodges, Vision Quests, dreamwork, and mining inner gold by looking deeply into his *shadows* of living and archetypal hardwiring.

Throughout his lifetime, Windancer has met with three near-death experiences through drowning, poisoning, and electrocution, which provided his belly's fire to know himself better. Looking backward at his life, Windancer holds immense gratitude for the process of his living, which involved a four-year stretch in the Marine Corps. Ceremony, ritual, and dreamwork are a large component of his living experience. He takes great joy in facilitating others into a mythological journey for creating greater versions of themselves. His greatest accomplishment however is to have married his soulmate and long-time dance partner. Together they have created the sacred space of covenantal bliss.